CLASSIC
CHINESE
COOKING

CLASSIC CHINESE COOKING

TEMPTING TASTES
FROM THE EAST

Consulting Editor: Linda Doeser

Sebastian Kelly

First published in 1999 by
Sebastian Kelly

Produced by Anness Publishing Limited

ISBN 1 84081 257 5

Publisher: Joanna Lorenz
Project Editor: Linda Doeser
Copy Editor: Harriet Lanzer
Designers: Ian Sandom, Siân Keogh

Front cover: Lisa Tai, Designer; Thomas Odulate, Photographer;
Helen Trent, Stylist; Lucy McKelvie, Home Economist

Photography: Karl Adamson, Edward Allwright, David Armstrong, Steve Baxter,
James Duncan, Michelle Garrett, Amanda Heywood, Patrick McLeavey,
William Lingwood, Michael Michaels and Thomas Odulate
Additional recipes: Kathy Man
Styling: Madeleine Brehaut, Michelle Garrett, Claire Louise Hunt, Maria Kelly,
Blake Minton and Kirsty Rawlings
Food for Photography: Carla Capalbo, Kit Chan, Joanne Craig, Nicola Fowler,
Carole Handslip, Jane Hartshorn, Wendy Lee, Lucy McKelvie, Annie Nichols,
Jane Stevenson, Steven Wheeler and Elizabeth Wolf-Cohen,
Illustrations: Madeleine David

Previously published as part of a larger compendium, *The Ultimate Chinese & Asian Cookbook*

Printed in Hong Kong/China

1 3 5 7 9 10 8 6 4 2

NOTES
All standard spoon and cup measurements are level.
Medium eggs should be used unless otherwise stated.

CONTENTS

INTRODUCTION

China is a vast country with many different regions. For nearly one thousand years, the northern city of Peking (now Beijing) has been the capital. Visiting dignitaries brought their chefs and culinary traditions from other parts of China. Through a mixture of co-operation and rivalry, they developed a light and elegant *haute cuisine*. Peking Duck must be the best-known specialty of the region.

Cantonese cooking in the South is colorful and sophisticated, based on abundant fresh vegetables, fish and seafood. Stir-frying was perfected here, and Canton is the home of Dim Sum, which literally means "to please the heart," and this describes the Cantonese approach to food.

Eastern Chinese cuisine divides into several styles. North of the Yangtze delta is famous for noodles and dumplings and is the home of the renowned Lion's Head Casserole. The southern provinces are known as the "Land of Fish and Rice," although their cuisine also includes many duck and pork dishes. The port of Shanghai has a unique style, influenced by the West as well as many parts of China.

The cuisine of Szechuan in the West of China is well-known for its superb balance of spices and aromatic flavorings. Chilies and Szechuan peppercorns are important and dishes are typically piquant and full of zest.

What all the classic dishes of the regional cuisines have in common is a harmonious balance of flavors, colors and textures and a long tradition of excellence.

THE WOK

There are many different varieties of wok available. All are bowl-shaped, with gently sloping sides that allow the heat to spread rapidly and evenly over the surface. One that is about 14 inches in diameter is a useful size for most families, allowing adequate room for deep-frying, steaming and braising, as well as stir-frying.

Originally always made from cast iron, woks are now manufactured in a number of different metals. Cast iron remains very popular, as it is an excellent conductor of heat and develops a patina over a period of time that makes it virtually nonstick. Carbon steel is also a good choice, but stainless steel tends to scorch. Nonstick woks are available but are not really very efficient because they cannot withstand the high heat required for wok cooking. They are also expensive.

Woks may have an ear-shaped handle made from metal or wood, a single long handle or both. Wooden handles are safer.

SEASONING THE WOK

New woks, apart from those with a nonstick lining, must be seasoned. Many need to be scrubbed first with dishwashing liquid to remove the manufacturer's protective coating of oil. Once the oil has been removed, place the wok over low heat and add about 2 tablespoons vegetable oil. Rub the oil over the entire inside surface of the wok with a pad of paper towels. Heat the wok slowly for 10 to 15 minutes, then wipe off the oil with more paper towels. The paper will become black. Repeat this process of coating, heating and wiping several times until the paper toweling is clean.

Once the wok has been seasoned, it should not be scrubbed again. After use, just wash it in hot water without using any detergent, then wipe it completely dry before storage. A wok in frequent use will not rust. However, if it does, scour off the rust and repeat the seasoning process.

WOK ACCESSORIES

There is a range of accessories available to go with woks, but they are by no means essential.

LID

This is a useful addition, particularly if you want to use the wok for steaming and braising, as well as frying. Usually made of aluminum, it is a close-fitting, dome-shaped cover. Some woks are sold already supplied with matching lids. However, any snug-fitting, dome-shaped saucepan lid is an adequate substitute.

STAND

This is used to provide a secure base for the wok when it is used for steaming, braising or deep-frying and is a particularly useful accessory. Stands are always made of metal but vary in form, and are usually either a simple open-sided frame or a solid metal ring with holes punched around the sides.

TRIVET

This is essential for steaming to support the plate above the water level. Trivets are made of wood or metal.

SCOOP

This is a long, often wooden-handled metal spatula with a wooden end used to toss ingredients during stir-frying. Any good, long-handled spoon can be used instead, although it does not have quite the same action.

Additional equipment is not essential for cooking with a wok, but utensils designed with this in mind—and tried and tested over time—can sometimes make the process easier. Wire and stainless steel skimmers, a wok scoop, a trivet and a selection of bamboo steamers in various sizes are among the most useful. Chinese cleavers are beautifully balanced cutting tools that can be used for both coarse and fine chopping. However, the range of cooking equipment found in most western kitchens can usually provide adequate substitutes for traditional Chinese tools and utensils.

WOK BRUSH

This bundle of stiff split bamboo is used for cleaning the wok. An ordinary kitchen brush is quite adequate.

OTHER EQUIPMENT

Most equipment required for cooking the recipes in this book will be found in any kitchen. Any specialized tools are generally simple and inexpensive, especially if you seek out authentic implements from Asian stores.

BAMBOO STEAMER

This fits inside the wok, where it should rest safely perched on the

sloping sides. Bamboo steamers range in size from small, for dumplings and dim sum, to those large enough to hold a whole fish.

BAMBOO STRAINER
This wide, flat, metal strainer with a long bamboo handle makes lifting foods from steam or hot oil easier. A slotted metal spoon can also be used.

CHOPSTICKS
Extra-long wooden chopsticks are useful for stirring, fluffing up rice, separating noodles during cooking and turning and transferring items.

CLEAVER
No Chinese cook would be without one. This is an all-purpose cutting tool, available in various weights and sizes. It is easy to use and serves many purposes, from chopping up bones to precision cutting, such as deveining shrimp. It is a superb instrument for thinly slicing vegetables. It must be kept very sharp.

CHINESE GRATER
These are typically made of wood.

KARAHI PAN
Also called a Balti pan, this is the Indian equivalent of a wok and is used in much the same way. A new Karahi pan should be seasoned in the same way as a new wok.

MORTAR AND PESTLE
Usually made of earthenware, this is extremely useful for grinding small amounts of spices and for pounding ingredients together to make pastes.

FOOD PROCESSOR
This is a quick and easy alternative to the mortar and pestle for grinding spices. It can also be used for chopping and slicing vegetables.

COOKING TECHNIQUES

STIR-FRYING

This quick technique retains the fresh flavor, color and texture of ingredients. Its success depends upon having all that you require ready before starting to cook.

1 Heat an empty wok over high heat. This prevents food from sticking and will ensure even heat. Add the oil and swirl it around so that it coats the base and halfway up the sides of the wok. It is important that the oil is hot when the food is added, so that it will start to cook immediately.

2 Add the ingredients in the order specified in the recipe: usually aromatics first (garlic, ginger, scallions). If this is the case, do not wait for the oil to get so hot that it is almost smoking or they will burn and become bitter. Toss them in the oil for a few seconds. Next add the main ingredients that require longer cooking, such as dense vegetables or meat. Follow with the faster-cooking items. Toss the ingredients from the center of the wok to the sides using a wok scoop, long-handled spoon or wooden spatula.

DEEP-FRYING

A wok is ideal for deep-frying, as it uses far less oil than a deep-fat fryer. Make sure that it is fully secure on its stand before adding the oil and never leave the wok unattended.

1 Put the wok on a stand and half fill with oil. Heat until the required temperature registers on a thermometer. Alternatively, test it by dropping in a small piece of food; if bubbles form all over the surface of the food, the oil is ready.

2 Carefully add the food to the oil, using wooden chopsticks or tongs, and move it around to prevent it from sticking together. Use a bamboo strainer or slotted spoon to remove the food. Drain on paper towels before serving.

STEAMING

Steamed foods are cooked by gentle, moist heat that must circulate freely in order for the food to cook. Steaming is increasingly popular with health-conscious cooks, as it preserves flavor and nutrients. It is perfect for vegetables, meat, poultry and especially fish. The easiest way to steam food in a wok is by using a bamboo steamer.

USING A BAMBOO STEAMER

1 Put the wok on a stand. Pour in sufficient boiling water to come about 2 inches up the sides and bring back to simmering point. Carefully place the bamboo steamer in the wok so that it rests securely against the sloping sides without touching the surface of the water.

2 Cover the steamer with its matching lid and cook for the time recommended in the recipe. Check the water level from time to time and add more boiling water if necessary.

USING A WOK AS A STEAMER

1 Put a trivet in the wok, then place the wok securely on its stand. Pour in sufficient boiling water to come just below the trivet. Carefully place a plate containing the food to be steamed on the trivet.

2 Cover the wok with its lid, bring the water back to a boil, then lower the heat so that it is simmering gently. Steam for the time recommended in the recipe. Check the water level from time to time and add boiling water if necessary.

INGREDIENTS

BAMBOO SHOOTS
These mild-flavored tender shoots of the young bamboo are widely available fresh, or sliced or halved in cans.

BEAN SPROUTS
These shoots of the mung bean are usually available at supermarkets. They add a crisp texture to stir-fries.

1 Pick over the bean sprouts and discard any that are discolored, broken or wilted.

2 Rinse the bean sprouts under cold running water and drain well.

CHINESE FIVE-SPICE POWDER
This flavoring contains star anise, pepper, fennel, cloves and cinnamon.

CHINESE PANCAKES
These unseasoned flour-and-water pancakes are available fresh or frozen.

CHINESE RICE VINEGAR
There are two basic types: red vinegar is made from fermented rice and is dark colored; white vinegar is distilled from rice and has a stronger flavor.

CREAMED COCONUT
This is available in solid blocks at Asian food stores and large supermarkets. It gives an intense coconut flavor; simply add water to make a thick coconut paste. It can be thinned with more water if required.

GINGER
Ginger has a sharp, distinctive flavor. Choose firm, plump pieces of fresh root with unwrinkled, shiny skins.

1 Using a small sharp knife, peel the skin from the root.

2 Place the ginger on a board. Set the flat side of a cleaver or chef's knife on top and strike it firmly with your fist to soften its fibrous texture.

3 Chop the ginger as coarsely or finely as you wish, moving the blade backward and forward.

GRAM FLOUR
Made from ground chickpeas, this flour has a unique flavor and is worth seeking out at Indian food stores.

KAFFIR LIME LEAVES
These are used rather like bay leaves, but to give an aromatic lime flavor to dishes. The fresh leaves are available at Asian food stores and can be frozen for future use.

1 Using a small, sharp knife, remove the center vein.

2 Cut the leaves horizontally into very fine strips.

LEMONGRASS
This herb imparts a mild, sour-sweet, citrus flavor. Split and use whole, finely chopped or ground to a paste.

DAIKON
Daikon is a member of the radish family with a fresh, slightly peppery taste. Unlike other radishes, it is good when cooked, but should be salted and allowed to drain first, as it has a high water content. It is widely used in Chinese cooking and may be carved into an elaborate garnish.

OKRA
This edible seedpod is a member of the hibiscus family and is also known as bhindi, gumbo and ladies' fingers. It is widely used in Indian cuisine.

OYSTER SAUCE
Made from oyster extract, it is used in many fish dishes, soups and sauces.

PLUM SAUCE
This is a sweet-and-sour sauce with a unique fruity flavor.

RED BEAN PASTE
This reddish-brown paste is made from puréed red beans and crystallized sugar. It is usually sold in cans.

RICE
Long-grain rice is generally used for savory dishes. There are many high-quality varieties, from a range of countries. Basmati, which means "fragrant" in Hindi, is generally acknowledged as the prince or king of rices and is probably the ideal choice for Indian recipes that suggest serving the dish with rice. Thai jasmine rice is also fragrant and slightly sticky.

RICE WINE
Made from glutinous rice, Chinese rice wine is also known as yellow wine—*huang jiu* or *chiew*—because of its color. The best variety is called *shao hsing* or *shaoxing* and comes from southeast China. Dry or medium sherry may be used as substitute.

SALTED BLACK BEANS
Sold in plastic bags and jars, these very

salty and pungent beans should be crushed with water or wine before use. They will keep almost indefinitely in a screw-top jar.

SESAME OIL
This is used more for flavoring than for cooking. It is very intensely flavored so only a little is required.

SHALLOTS
Mild-flavored members of the onion family, shallots are used in many flavorings and sauces. Fried in crisp flakes, they can be used as a garnish.

SPRING ONIONS
These are widely used in stir-fried dishes. The thinner the onion, the milder it will be. Chop off any roots and the top part of the green section, then chop finely or cut into matchstick strips. In some recipes, the green and white parts are kept separate for an extra decorative effect.

Cockwise from top left: yellow bean sauce, black bean sauce, oyster sauce, dark soy sauce, light soy sauce, and hoisin sauce.

Remove and discard the woody stalks from soaked, dried Chinese mushrooms, then use the caps whole, sliced, or chopped.

SHIITAKE MUSHROOMS
Dried shiitake mushrooms, widely known as Chinese dried mushrooms, are frequently used in classic Chinese cuisine. They have a more concentrated flavor than fresh mushrooms. They should be soaked in hot water before use for about 30 minutes, until softened. Remove and discard the stalks and use the caps whole, sliced or chopped, according to the recipe.

SOY SAUCE
Made from the naturally fermented soy bean, this is an important ingredient in Chinese cooking. There are two types: dark and light. Dark soy sauce is rich and used to add both color and flavor to many sauces and marinades. It is quite salty and is often used instead of salt to season a dish. Light soy sauce is thinner, lighter, and has a fresher taste than dark. It is also saltier. It is used in cooking, as a table condiment, and as a dipping sauce.

SPRING ROLL SKINS OR WRAPPERS
Paper-thin wrappers made from wheat or rice flour and water, they are available from Chinese supermarkets. Wheat wrappers are usually sold frozen and should be thawed and separated before use. Rice flour wrappers are dry and must be soaked before use.

STRAW MUSHROOMS
These are grown on rice straw and have a slippery texture, for which they are prized, but little flavor. They are available canned from supermarkets and Chinese food stores. They are not widely available fresh in the West.

Often used to add texture and color contrast in stir-fried meat and fish dishes, wood ears must be soaked before use. Then discard the woody stems and slice thinly.

WATER CHESTNUTS

This walnut-size bulb comes from an Asian water plant and looks like a sweet chestnut, although the two plants are not related. They are sold fresh by some Chinese supermarkets, but are usually more readily available canned.

WONTON WRAPPERS

These paper-thin squares of yellow-colored dough are available from most Chinese supermarkets.

WOOD EARS

Dried edible fungi that have a crunchy texture, wood ears are widely available from Chinese supermarkets. Cloud ears, which are similar but with a more delicate flavour, are sometimes a little more difficult to obtain. Once reconstituted in water, they expand to many times their original size. They should be soaked in hot water before use for 30 minutes, or until softened. Drain, rinse, and cut them into small pieces, discarding the tough base.

YELLOW BEAN SAUCE

This thick paste is made from salted, fermented, yellow soy beans, crushed with flour and sugar.

SZECHUAN PEPPERCORNS

Also known as farchiew, these aromatic red peppercorns are best used roasted and ground. They are not so hot as either white or black peppercorns, but do add a unique taste to food.

TOFU

Also known as bean curd, tofu is used extensively in Chinese cooking and is a good source of protein, especially for vegetarians. Although it is very bland, indeed almost flavorless, tofu readily absorbs the flavors of the food with which it is cooked. Firm blocks of tofu are best suited to stir-frying. Store, covered with water, in the refrigerator.

Clockwise from top: fresh bean curd or tofu, dried bean curd sticks and aduki beans – just some of the protein-rich components of many Chinese recipes.

Tofu is readily available from supermarkets and health food stores. There are several other different types, including "silken" and smoked. Dried bean curd sticks are sheets of tofu that have been formed into sticks and dried. They are an important ingredient in Chinese vegetarian dishes. They must be soaked in hot water before being used. Bean curd sticks are usually available from Chinese foodstores.

SOUPS &
APPETIZERS

Chicken Wonton Soup with Shrimp

This soup is a more luxurious version of the familiar, basic wonton soup and is almost a meal in itself.

INGREDIENTS

Serves 4

10 ounces boneless chicken
   breast, skinned
7 ounces jumbo shrimp, raw or cooked
1 teaspoon finely chopped fresh ginger
2 scallions, finely chopped
1 egg
2 teaspoons oyster sauce (optional)
1 packet wonton wrappers
1 tablespoon cornstarch paste
3¾ cups chicken broth
¼ cucumber, peeled and diced
salt and freshly ground black pepper
1 scallion, cut into strips
4 sprigs fresh cilantro and 1 tomato,
   skinned, seeded and diced, to garnish

1 Place the chicken breast, three-quarters of the shrimp, the ginger and scallions in a food processor and process for 2–3 minutes. Add the egg, oyster sauce, if using, and seasoning and process briefly. Set aside.

2 Place 8 wonton wrappers at a time on a surface, moisten the edges with cornstarch paste and place ½ teaspoon of the chicken mixture in the center of each. Fold them in half and pinch to seal. Simmer in salted water for 4 minutes.

3 Bring the chicken broth to a boil, add the remaining shrimp and the cucumber and simmer for 3–4 minutes. Add the filled wontons and simmer for 3–4 minutes to warm through. Garnish with the scallion, cilantro and diced tomato and serve hot.

Corn and Chicken Soup

This popular, classic Chinese soup is delicious and extremely easy to make in a wok.

INGREDIENTS

Serves 4-6
1 boneless chicken breast (about 4 ounces), skinned and cubed
2 teaspoons light soy sauce
1 tablespoon Chinese rice wine or dry sherry
1 teaspoon cornstarch
¼ cup cold water
1 teaspoon sesame oil
2 tablespoons peanut oil
1 teaspoon grated fresh ginger
4 cups chicken stock
15-ounce can creamed corn
8-ounce can corn kernels
2 eggs, beaten
salt and ground black pepper
2–3 scallions, green parts only, cut into tiny rounds, to garnish

1 Grind the chicken in a food processor or blender, taking care not to overprocess. Transfer the chicken to a bowl and stir in the soy sauce, rice wine or sherry, cornstarch, water, sesame oil and seasoning. Cover and let sit for about 15 minutes to absorb the flavors.

2 Heat a wok over medium heat. Add the peanut oil and swirl it around. Add the ginger and stir-fry for a few seconds. Add the stock, creamed corn and corn kernels. Bring to just below boiling point.

3 Spoon about 6 tablespoons of the hot liquid into the chicken mixture and stir until it forms a smooth paste. Add to the wok. Slowly bring to a boil, stirring constantly, then simmer for 2–3 minutes, until cooked.

4 Pour the beaten eggs into the soup in a slow, steady stream, using a fork or chopsticks to stir the top of the soup in a figure-eight pattern. The egg should set in lacy threads. Serve immediately with the scallions sprinkled on top.

Beef Noodle Soup

A steaming bowl, packed with delicious flavors and a taste of the Orient, will be welcome on cold winter days.

INGREDIENTS

Serves 4

¼ ounce dried porcini mushrooms
⅔ cup boiling water
6 scallions
2 medium carrots
12 ounces sirloin steak
about 2 tablespoons sunflower oil
1 garlic clove, crushed
1-inch piece fresh ginger, peeled and finely chopped
5 cups beef broth
3 tablespoons light soy sauce
4 tablespoons Chinese rice wine or dry sherry
3 ounces thin egg noodles
3 ounces spinach, shredded
salt and freshly ground black pepper

3 Heat the oil in a large saucepan and brown the beef in batches, adding a little more oil if necessary. Remove the beef with a slotted spoon and set aside to drain on paper towels.

4 Add the garlic, ginger, scallions and carrots to the pan and stir-fry for 3 minutes.

5 Add the beef broth, the mushrooms and their soaking liquid, the soy sauce, rice wine or dry sherry and plenty of seasoning. Bring to a boil and simmer, covered, for 10 minutes.

6 Break up the noodles slightly and add to the pan with the spinach. Simmer gently for 5 minutes, or until the beef is tender. Adjust the seasoning before serving.

1 Break the mushrooms into small pieces, place in a bowl and pour the boiling water over them. Set aside to soak for 15 minutes.

2 Shred the scallions and carrots into fine 2-inch-long strips. Trim any fat off the steak and slice into thin strips.

Clear Soup with Meatballs

INGREDIENTS

Serves 8

For the meatballs

6 ounces very finely ground beef
1 small onion, very finely chopped
1–2 garlic cloves, crushed
1 tablespoon cornstarch
a little egg white, lightly beaten
salt and freshly ground black pepper

For the soup

4–6 Chinese mushrooms, soaked in
   warm water for 30 minutes
2 tablespoons peanut oil
1 large onion, finely chopped
2 garlic cloves, finely crushed
½ inch fresh ginger root, bruised
8 cups beef or chicken broth, including
   strained soaking liquid from
   the mushrooms
2 tablespoons soy sauce
4 ounces spinach or Chinese
   cabbage, shredded

1 First prepare the meatballs. Mix the beef with the onion, garlic, cornstarch and seasoning in a food processor and then bind with sufficient egg white to make a firm mixture. With dampened hands, roll into tiny, bite-size balls and set aside.

2 Drain the mushrooms and reserve the soaking liquid to add to the broth. Trim off and discard the stalks. Slice the caps finely and set aside.

3 Heat a large saucepan or wok and add the oil. Fry the onion, garlic and ginger to bring out the flavor, but do not allow to brown.

4 When the onion is soft, pour in the broth. Bring to a boil, then stir in the soy sauce and mushroom slices and simmer for 10 minutes. Add the meatballs and cook for 10 minutes.

5 Just before serving, remove the ginger. Stir in the shredded spinach or Chinese cabbage. Heat through for 1 minute only: no longer or the leaves will be overcooked. Serve the soup immediately.

Chicken and Asparagus Soup

This is a very delicate soup, with chicken and asparagus simply and quickly prepared in a wok.

INGREDIENTS

Serves 4
1 boneless chicken breast (about 5 ounces), skinned
1 teaspoon egg white
1 teaspoon cornstarch paste
½ bunch fresh asparagus (about 4 ounces)
3 cups chicken stock
salt and ground black pepper
fresh cilantro, to garnish

1 Cut the chicken into thin slices, each about the size of a postage stamp. Mix with a pinch of salt, then add the egg white and finally the cornstarch paste.

2 Discard the tough stems of the asparagus, and cut the tender spears diagonally into short lengths.

3 Bring the stock to a rolling boil in a wok. Add the asparagus, bring back to a boil and cook for 2 minutes.

4 Add the chicken, stir to separate and bring back to a boil again. Adjust the seasoning to taste. Serve hot, garnished with fresh cilantro leaves.

Crab Spring Rolls and Dipping Sauce

Chili and grated ginger add a hint of heat to these sensational treats. Serve them as an appetizer or with other Chinese dishes as part of a main course.

INGREDIENTS

Serves 4–6

1 tablespoon peanut oil
1 teaspoon sesame oil
1 garlic clove, crushed
1 fresh red chili, seeded and finely sliced
1 pound fresh stir-fry vegetables, such as bean sprouts and shredded carrots, bell peppers and snow peas
2 tablespoons chopped cilantro
1-inch piece fresh ginger, grated
1 tablespoon Chinese rice wine or dry sherry
1 tablespoon soy sauce
12 ounces fresh dressed crabmeat (brown and white meat)
12 spring roll wrappers
1 small egg, beaten
oil, for deep-frying
salt and freshly ground black pepper
lime wedges and fresh cilantro, to garnish

For the dipping sauce

1 onion, thinly sliced
oil, for deep-frying
1 fresh red chili, seeded and finely chopped
2 garlic cloves, crushed
4 tablespoons dark soy sauce
4 teaspoons lemon juice or 1–1½ tablespoons prepared tamarind juice
2 tablespoons hot water

1 First make the sauce. Spread the onion out on paper towels and let dry for 30 minutes. Then half-fill a wok with oil and heat to 375°F. Fry the onion in batches until crisp and golden, turning all the time. Drain on paper towels.

2 Combine the chili, garlic, soy sauce, lemon or tamarind juice and hot water in a bowl.

3 Stir in the onion and let stand for 30 minutes.

4 To make the spring rolls, heat the peanut and sesame oils in a clean, preheated wok. When hot, stir-fry the crushed garlic and chili for 1 minute. Add the vegetables, cilantro and ginger and stir-fry for 1 minute more. Drizzle with the rice wine or dry sherry and soy sauce. Allow the mixture to bubble up for 1 minute.

5 Using a slotted spoon, transfer the vegetables to a bowl. Set aside until cool, then stir in the crabmeat and season with salt and pepper.

6 Soften the spring roll wrappers, following the directions on the package. Place some of the filling on a wrapper, fold over the front edge and the sides, and roll up neatly, sealing the edges with a little beaten egg. Repeat with the remaining wrappers and filling.

7 Heat the oil for deep-frying in the wok and fry the spring rolls in batches, turning several times, until brown and crisp. Remove with a slotted spoon, drain on paper towels and keep hot while frying the remainder. Serve at once, garnished with lime wedges and cilantro, with the dipping sauce.

Butterfly Shrimp

For best results, use uncooked jumbo shrimp in their shells for this deep-fried dish. Sold headless, they are about 3–4 inches long, and you should get 18–20 shrimp per pound.

INGREDIENTS

Serves 6–8

1 pound uncooked shrimp in their
   shells, heads removed
1 teaspoon ground Szechuan
   peppercorns
1 tablespoon light soy sauce
1 tablespoon Chinese rice wine or
   dry sherry
2 teaspoons cornstarch
2 eggs, lightly beaten
4–5 tablespoons bread crumbs
vegetable oil, for deep-frying
2–3 scallions, to garnish
lettuce leaves, to serve

1 Shell the shrimp but leave the tails on. Butterfly the shrimp, about three-quarters of the way through their length, leaving the tails still firmly attached.

2 Put the shrimp in a bowl with the pepper, soy sauce, rice wine or sherry and cornstarch and set aside to marinate for 10–15 minutes.

3 Pick up one shrimp at a time by the tail, and dip it in the beaten egg.

4 Roll the egg-covered shrimp in bread crumbs.

5 Heat the oil in a wok until medium-hot. Gently lower the shrimp into the oil.

6 Deep-fry the shrimp in batches until golden brown. Remove and drain. To serve, arrange the shrimp neatly on a bed of lettuce leaves. Garnish with scallions, either raw or after soaking for about 30 seconds in hot oil.

Steamed Pork and Water Chestnut Wontons

Ginger and Chinese five-spice powder flavor this version of steamed dumplings—a favorite snack in many teahouses.

INGREDIENTS

Makes about 36

2 large Chinese cabbage leaves, plus extra for lining the steamer
2 scallions, finely chopped
½-inch piece fresh ginger, chopped
2 ounces canned water chestnuts, rinsed and finely chopped
8 ounces ground pork
½ teaspoon Chinese five-spice powder
1 tablespoon cornstarch
1 tablespoon light soy sauce
1 tablespoon Chinese rice wine or dry sherry
2 teaspoons sesame oil
generous pinch of superfine sugar
about 36 wonton wrappers, each 3 inches square
light soy sauce and hot chili oil, for dipping

1 Place the Chinese cabbage leaves one on top of the other. Cut them lengthwise into quarters and then across into thin shreds.

2 Place the shredded Chinese cabbage leaves in a bowl. Add the scallions, ginger, water chestnuts, pork, five-spice powder, cornstarch, soy sauce, rice wine or dry sherry, sesame oil and sugar and mix well.

3 Place a heaped teaspoon of the filling in the center of a wrapper. Lightly dampen the edges with water.

4 Lift the wrapper up around the filling, gathering it to form a "purse." Squeeze the wrapper firmly around the middle, then tap the bottom to make a flat base. The top should be open. Place the wonton on a tray and cover with a damp kitchen towel. Repeat until the filling is used up.

5 Line a steamer with cabbage leaves and steam the dumplings for 12–15 minutes, or until tender. Remove each batch from the steamer as soon they are cooked, cover with foil and keep warm. Serve hot with soy sauce and chili oil for dipping.

Dim Sum

Popular as a snack in China, these tiny dumplings are fast becoming fashionable in many restaurants in the West.

INGREDIENTS

Serves 4

For the dough
1¼ cups all–purpose flour
¼ cup boiling water
1½ tablespoons cold water
½ tablespoon vegetable oil

For the filling
3 ounces ground pork
3 tablespoons canned chopped
   bamboo shoots
½ tablespoon light soy sauce
1 teaspoon dry sherry
1 teaspoon light brown sugar
½ teaspoon sesame oil
1 teaspoon cornstarch
lettuce leaves such as iceberg or frisée,
   soy sauce, scallion curls, sliced fresh
   red chili and shrimp crackers,
   to serve

2 Divide the mixture into 16 equal pieces and shape into circles.

3 For the filling, mix together the pork, bamboo shoots, soy sauce, dry sherry, sugar and oil.

5 Place a little of the filling in the center of each dim sum circle. Pinch the edges of the dough together to form little "purses."

6 Line a steamer with a damp kitchen towel. Place the dim sum in the steamer and steam for 5–10 minutes. Arrange the lettuce leaves on four individual serving plates, top with the dim sum and serve with soy sauce, scallion curls, sliced red chili and shrimp crackers.

1 To make the dough, sift the flour into a bowl. Stir in the boiling water, then the cold water together with the oil. Mix to form a dough, turn out onto a lightly floured surface, and knead until smooth.

4 Add the cornstarch and stir well until thoroughly combined.

VARIATION

You can replace the pork with cooked, peeled shrimp. Sprinkle 1 tablespoon sesame seeds over the dim sum before cooking, if desired.

Deep-fried Ribs with Spicy Salt and Pepper

INGREDIENTS

Serves 4–6
10–12 pork spareribs (about 1¹/₂ pounds),
 excess fat trimmed
2–3 tablespoons flour
vegetable oil, for deep-frying
scallion tassels, to garnish (optional)

For the marinade
1 clove garlic, crushed
1 tablespoon light brown sugar
1 tablespoon light soy sauce
1 tablespoon dark soy sauce
2 tablespoons Chinese rice wine or
 dry sherry
¹/₂ teaspoon chili sauce
few drops of sesame oil

For the spicy salt and pepper
1 tablespoon salt
2 teaspoons ground Szechuan
 peppercorns
1 teaspoon five-spice powder

1 Chop each rib into three or four pieces, then mix with all the marinade ingredients and marinate for at least 2–3 hours.

COOK'S TIP

Ideally, each sparerib should be chopped into three or four bite-size pieces before or after deep-frying in a wok. If this is not possible, serve the ribs whole.

2 Coat the ribs with flour and deep-fry in medium-hot oil for 4–5 minutes, stirring to separate. Remove from the oil and drain.

3 Heat the oil to high and deep-fry the ribs again for about 1 minute or until the color is an even dark brown. Remove and drain.

4 To make the spicy salt and pepper, heat all the ingredients in a preheated dry wok for about 2 minutes over low heat, stirring constantly. Serve with the ribs. Garnish the dish with scallion tassels, if desired.

Bon-bon Chicken with Sesame Sauce

The chicken meat is tenderized by being beaten with a stick (called a *bon* in Chinese), hence the name for this very popular Szechuan dish.

INGREDIENTS

Serves 6–8
1 chicken (about 3 pounds)
5 cups water
1 tablespoon sesame oil
shredded cucumber, to garnish

For the sauce
2 tablespoons light soy sauce
1 teaspoon sugar
1 tablespoon finely chopped scallions
1 teaspoon red chili oil
$^{1}/_{2}$ teaspoon ground Szechuan peppercorns
1 teaspoon white sesame seeds
2 tablespoons tahini or 2 tablespoons peanut butter creamed with a little sesame oil

1 Clean the chicken well. Bring the water to a rolling boil in a wok and add the chicken. Reduce the heat, cover and cook for 40–45 minutes. Remove the chicken and immerse in cold water to cool.

2 After at least 1 hour, remove the chicken and drain; dry well with paper towels and brush on a coating of sesame oil. Carve the meat off the legs, wings and breast and pull the meat off the rest of the bones.

3 On a flat surface, pound the meat with a rolling pin, then tear it into shreds with your fingers.

4 Place the meat in a dish with the shredded cucumber around the edge. In a bowl, combine all the sauce ingredients, keeping the scallions to garnish. Pour the sauce over the chicken, garnish and serve.

FISH & SHELLFISH

Gong Boa Shrimp

This pleasantly spicy sweet-and-sour shrimp dish takes only minutes to make.

INGREDIENTS

Serves 4

12 ounces raw jumbo shrimp
½ cucumber, about 3 ounces
1¼ cups fish stock
1 tablespoon vegetable oil
½ teaspoon crushed dried chilies
½ green bell pepper, seeded and cut
   into 1-inch strips
1 small carrot, thinly sliced
2 tablespoons tomato ketchup
3 tablespoons rice vinegar
1 tablespoon superfine sugar
⅔ cup vegetable stock
½ cup drained canned
   pineapple chunks
2 teaspoons cornstarch
1 tablespoon cold water
salt

1 Peel and devein the shrimp. Rub them gently with ½ teaspoon salt. Leave them for a few minutes, then wash and dry thoroughly.

2 Pare strips of skin off the cucumber to give a stripy effect. Cut the cucumber in half lengthwise and scoop out the seeds with a teaspoon. Cut the flesh into ¼-inch crescents.

3 Bring the fish stock to a boil in a saucepan. Add the shrimp, lower the heat, and poach them for about 2 minutes, until they turn pink. Drain the shrimp and set aside.

4 Heat the oil in a preheated wok or skillet. Add the chilies and stir-fry for a few seconds, then add the bell pepper strips and carrot slices, and stir-fry for 1 minute.

5 Mix together the tomato ketchup, vinegar, sugar, and vegetable stock, and season with salt. Pour the mixture into the wok or skillet and cook for 3 minutes.

6 Add the shrimp, cucumber, and pineapple and cook for 2 minutes. Mix together the cornstarch and water to a smooth paste. Add the mixture to the wok or skillet and cook, stirring constantly, until the sauce has thickened. Serve at once.

Baked Crab with Scallions and Ginger

This recipe is far less complicated than it looks and will delight the eye as much as the taste buds.

INGREDIENTS

Serves 4

1 large or 2 medium crabs, about 1½ pounds total
2 tablespoons Chinese rice wine or dry sherry
1 egg, lightly beaten
1 tablespoon cornstarch
3–4 tablespoons vegetable oil
1 tablespoon finely chopped fresh ginger
3–4 scallions, cut into short lengths
2 tablespoons soy sauce
1 teaspoon light brown sugar
about 5 tablespoons Basic Broth
few drops of sesame oil

1 Cut the crab in half from the underbelly. Break off the claws and crack them with the back of a cleaver. Discard the legs and crack the shell, breaking it into several pieces. Discard the feathery gills and the sac. Put the pieces of crab in a bowl.

2 Combine the rice wine or dry sherry, egg and cornstarch and pour over the crab. Marinate for 10–15 minutes.

3 Heat the oil in a preheated wok. Add the crab pieces, ginger and scallions and stir-fry for 2 to 3 minutes.

4 Add the soy sauce, sugar and broth and blend well. Bring to a boil, reduce the heat, cover and braise for 3–4 minutes, or until it is cooked. Transfer the crab to a serving dish, sprinkle with the sesame oil and serve.

COOK'S TIP

For the very best flavor, buy a live crab and cook it yourself. However, if you prefer to buy a cooked crab, look for one that feels heavy for its size. This is an indication that it has fully grown into its shell and that there will be plenty of meat. Male crabs have larger claws and so will yield a greater proportion of white meat. However, females—identifiable by a broader, less pointed tail flap—may contain coral, which many people regard as a delicacy.

Spiced Scallops in their Shells

Scallops are excellent steamed. When served with this spicy sauce, they make a delicious, yet simple, appetizer for four people or a light lunch for two. Each person spoons sauce onto the scallops before eating them.

INGREDIENTS

Serves 2
8 scallops, shelled (ask the fishmonger to reserve the cupped side of 4 shells)
2 slices fresh ginger, shredded
½ garlic clove, shredded
2 scallions, green parts only, cut into fine strips
salt and freshly ground black pepper

For the sauce
1 garlic clove, crushed
1 tablespoon grated fresh ginger
2 scallions, white parts only, chopped
1–2 fresh green chilies, seeded and finely chopped
1 tablespoon light soy sauce
1 tablespoon dark soy sauce
2 teaspoons sesame oil

1 Remove the dark beardlike fringe and tough muscle from the scallops.

2 Place 2 scallops in each shell. Season lightly with salt and pepper, then scatter the ginger, garlic and scallions on top. Place the shells in a bamboo steamer in a wok and steam for about 6 minutes, or until the scallops look opaque (you may have to do this in batches).

3 Meanwhile, make the sauce. Mix together the garlic, ginger, scallions, chilies, soy sauces and sesame oil and pour into a small serving bowl.

4 Carefully remove each shell from the steamer, taking care not to spill the juices, and arrange them on a serving plate with the sauce bowl in the center. Serve at once.

Seafood Chow Mein

This basic recipe can be adapted using different items for the "dressing."

INGREDIENTS

Serves 4

3 ounces squid, cleaned
3 ounces jumbo shrimp
3–4 fresh scallops
½ egg white
1 tablespoon cornstarch paste
9 ounces egg noodles
5–6 tablespoons vegetable oil
2 ounces snow peas
½ teaspoon salt
½ teaspoon light brown sugar
1 tablespoon Chinese rice wine or
   dry sherry
2 tablespoons light soy sauce
2 scallions, cut into fine strips
Basic Broth, if necessary
few drops of sesame oil

1 Open up the squid and score the inside in a crisscross pattern with a sharp knife. Cut the squid into pieces, each about the size of a postage stamp. Soak the squid in a bowl of boiling water until all the pieces curl up. Rinse in cold water and drain.

2 Peel and devein the shrimp, then cut each in half lengthwise.

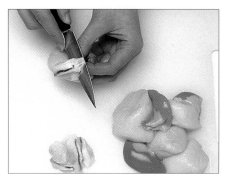

3 Prepare the scallops and cut into 3 or 4 slices. Combine the scallops, shrimp, egg white and cornstarch paste.

4 Cook the noodles in boiling water according to the package instructions. Drain and refresh under cold water. Mix with about 1 tablespoon of the oil.

5 Heat 2–3 tablespoons of the oil in a preheated wok. Stir-fry the snow peas, squid and shrimp mixture for about 2 minutes, then add the salt, sugar, rice wine or dry sherry, half the soy sauce and the scallions. Blend well and add a little broth, if necessary. Remove from the wok and keep warm.

6 Heat the remaining oil in the wok and stir-fry the noodles for 2–3 minutes with the remaining soy sauce. Place in a large serving dish, pour the "dressing" on top and sprinkle with a little sesame oil. Serve hot or cold.

Three Sea Flavors Stir-fry

This delectable seafood combination is enhanced by the use of fresh ginger root and scallions.

Ingredients

Serves 4

4 large scallops with corals
8 ounces firm white fish fillet, such as
   monkfish or cod
4 ounces raw jumbo shrimp
1¼ cups fish stock
1 tablespoon vegetable oil
2 garlic cloves, coarsely chopped
2-inch piece of fresh ginger root,
   thinly sliced
8 scallions, cut into
   1½-inch pieces
2 tablespoons Chinese rice wine
1 teaspoon cornstarch
1 tablespoon water
salt and freshly ground white pepper
noodles, to serve

1 Separate the corals from the scallops and slice each scallop in half horizontally. Cut the fish fillet into bite-size chunks. Peel and devein the jumbo shrimp.

2 Bring the fish stock to a boil in a saucepan. Add the seafood, lower the heat, and poach gently for 1–2 minutes, until the fish, scallops, and corals are just firm and the shrimp have turned pink. Drain the fish and seafood, reserving about 4 tablespoons of the stock, and set aside.

3 Heat the oil in a preheated wok or large skillet. Add the garlic, ginger, and scallions and stir-fry for a few seconds.

4 Add the seafood and wine and stir-fry for 1 minute. Add the reserved stock and simmer for 2 minutes.

5 Mix together the cornstarch and water to a smooth paste. Add the mixture to the wok or skillet and cook, stirring gently, until the sauce thickens.

6 Season with salt and pepper to taste. Transfer to a serving dish and serve at once with noodles.

Cook's Tip

Do not overcook the seafood or it will become rubbery.

Monkfish and Scallop Skewers

Using lemon grass stalks as skewers imbues the seafood with a subtle citrus flavor.

INGREDIENTS

Serves 4

1 pound monkfish fillet
8 lemon grass stalks
2 tablespoons fresh lemon juice
1 tablespoon olive oil
1 tablespoon finely chopped
   fresh cilantro
½ teaspoon salt
12 large scallops, cut in
   half crosswise
freshly ground black pepper
fresh cilantro sprigs, to garnish
rice, to serve

1 Remove the tough, transparent membrane from the monkfish, otherwise it will shrink during cooking. Cut the flesh into 16 large chunks with a sharp knife.

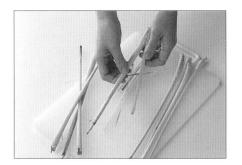

2 Remove the outer leaves from the lemon grass. Finely chop the tender parts of the leaves and place in a bowl. Stir in the lemon juice, olive oil, chopped cilantro, and salt and season to taste with pepper.

3 Thread the monkfish and scallop chunks on the eight lemon grass stalks. Arrange the skewers of fish and shellfish in a shallow dish and pour over the marinade, turning the skewers to coat thoroughly.

4 Cover and set aside for 1 hour. Transfer the skewers to a steamer, cover, and steam over boiling water for 10 minutes, until just cooked. Garnish with cilantro and serve with rice and the cooking juice poured over.

Fried Monkfish Coated with Rice Noodles

These marinated medallions of fish are coated in rice vermicelli and deep-fried – they taste as good as they look.

INGREDIENTS

Serves 4
1 pound monkfish
1 teaspoon grated fresh ginger
1 garlic clove, finely chopped
2 tablespoons soy sauce
6 ounces rice vermicelli
4 tablespoons cornstarch
2 eggs, beaten
salt and freshly ground black pepper
oil for deep-frying
banana leaves, to serve (optional)

For the dipping sauce
2 tablespoons soy sauce
2 tablespoons rice vinegar
1 tablespoon sugar
2 red chilies, thinly sliced
1 scallion, thinly sliced

1 Trim the monkfish, and cut into 1-inch thick medallions. Place in a dish, and add the ginger, garlic and soy sauce. Mix lightly, and let marinate for 10 minutes.

2 Meanwhile, make the dipping sauce. Combine the soy sauce, vinegar and sugar in a small saucepan. Bring to a boil. Add salt and pepper to taste. Remove from the heat, add the chilies and scallion, and then set aside until required.

3 Using kitchen scissors, cut the noodles into 1½-inch lengths. Spread them out in a shallow bowl.

4 Lightly coat the fish medallions in cornstarch, dip in beaten egg, and cover with noodles, pressing them on to the fish so that they stick.

5 Deep-fry the coated fish in hot oil, two to three pieces at a time, until the noodle coating is fluffy, crisp and light golden brown. Drain, and serve hot on banana leaves, if you like, accompanied by the dipping sauce.

Sizzling Chinese Steamed Fish

Steamed whole fish is very popular in China, where the wok is used as a steamer. In this recipe the fish is flavored with garlic, ginger and scallions cooked in sizzling hot oil.

INGREDIENTS

Serves 4

4 rainbow trout, about 9 ounces each
¼ teaspoon salt
½ teaspoon sugar
2 garlic cloves, finely chopped
1 tablespoon finely diced fresh ginger
5 scallions, cut into 2-inch lengths and
　　then into fine strips
¼ cup peanut oil
1 teaspoon sesame oil
3 tablespoons light soy sauce
thread egg noodles and stir-fried
　　vegetables, to serve

1 Make three diagonal slits on both sides of each fish and lay them on a heatproof plate. Place a small rack or trivet in a wok half-filled with water, cover and heat until just simmering.

2 Sprinkle the fish with the salt, sugar, garlic and ginger. Place the plate securely on the rack or trivet and cover. Steam gently for about 12 minutes, or until the flesh has turned pale pink and feels quite firm.

3 Turn off the heat, remove the lid and scatter the scallions over the fish. Replace the lid.

4 Heat the peanut and sesame oils in a small pan over high heat until just smoking, then quickly pour a quarter over the scallions on each of the fish—the scallions will sizzle and cook in the hot oil. Sprinkle the soy sauce over the top. Serve the fish and juices immediately with boiled noodles and stir-fried vegetables.

Sea Bass with Chinese Chives

Chinese chives are widely available in Asian supermarkets but if you are unable to buy them, use half a large Spanish onion, finely sliced, instead.

INGREDIENTS

Serves 4
2 sea bass, about 1 pound total
1 tablespoon cornstarch
3 tablespoons vegetable oil
6 ounces Chinese chives
1 tablespoon Chinese rice wine or
　dry sherry
1 teaspoon superfine sugar
salt and freshly ground black pepper
Chinese chives with flower heads,
　to garnish

1 Remove the scales from the bass by scraping them with the back of a knife, working from the tail end toward the head end. Fillet the fish. Your fishmonger could do this for you.

2 Cut the fillets into large chunks and dust them lightly with cornstarch, salt and pepper.

3 Heat 2 tablespoons of the oil in a preheated wok. When the oil is hot, toss the chunks of fish in the wok briefly to seal, then set aside. Wipe out the wok with paper towels.

4 Cut the Chinese chives into 2-inch lengths and discard the flowers. Reheat the wok and add the remaining oil, then stir-fry the Chinese chives for 30 seconds. Add the fish and rice wine or dry sherry, then bring to a boil and stir in the sugar. Serve hot, garnished with some flowering Chinese chives.

Gray Mullet with Pork

This unusual combination makes a spectacular main dish.

INGREDIENTS

Serves 4

1 gray mullet, about 2 pounds, gutted and cleaned
2 ounces lean pork
3 dried Chinese mushrooms, soaked in hot water for 30 minutes
½ teaspoon cornstarch
2 tablespoons light soy sauce
1 tablespoon vegetable oil
1 tablespoon finely shredded fresh ginger root
1 tablespoon shredded scallion
salt and freshly ground black pepper
sliced scallion, to garnish
rice, to serve

1 Make four diagonal cuts on either side of the fish and rub with a little salt. Place the fish on a large, shallow, heatproof serving dish.

2 Cut the pork into thin strips. Place in a bowl. Drain the soaked mushrooms, remove and discard the stalks and thinly slice the caps.

3 Add the mushrooms to the pork, together with the cornstarch and half the soy sauce. Stir in 1 teaspoon of the oil and season generously with black pepper. Arrange the pork mixture along the length of the fish. Scatter the ginger shreds over the top.

4 Cover the fish loosely with foil. Have ready a large saucepan or roasting pan with about 2 inches boiling water. (It should be big enough for the heatproof dish to fit inside on a metal trivet.) Place the dish in the pan or roasting pan, cover, and steam over high heat for 15 minutes.

5 Test the fish by pressing the flesh gently. If it comes away from the bone with a slight resistance, the fish is cooked. Carefully pour away any excess liquid from the dish.

6 Heat the remaining oil in a small pan. Add the shredded scallion and stir-fry for a few seconds, then pour it over the fish, taking great care as it will splatter. Drizzle with the remaining soy sauce, garnish with sliced scallion, and serve at once with rice.

MEAT &
POULTRY

Stir-fried Pork with Vegetables

This is a basic recipe for stir-frying any meat with any vegetables, according to seasonal availability and preference.

INGREDIENTS

Serves 4
8 ounces pork loin
1 tablespoon light soy sauce
1 teaspoon light brown sugar
1 teaspoon Chinese rice wine or
   dry sherry
2 teaspoons cornstarch paste
4 ounces snow peas
1½ cups white mushrooms
1 carrot
1 scallion
¼ cup vegetable oil
1 teaspoon salt
stock (optional)
few drops of sesame oil

1 Cut the pork into thin slices, each about the size of a postage stamp. Marinate with about 1 teaspoon of the soy sauce, and the sugar, wine or sherry and cornstarch paste.

2 Trim the snow peas. Thinly slice the mushrooms. Cut the carrot into pieces roughly the same size as the pork. Cut the scallion into short sections.

3 Heat the oil in a preheated wok and stir-fry the pork for about 1 minute or until its color changes. Remove with a slotted spoon and keep warm while you cook the vegetables.

4 Add the vegetables to the wok and stir-fry for about 2 minutes. Add the salt and the partly cooked pork, and a little stock if necessary. Continue cooking and stirring for about 1 minute, then add the remaining soy sauce and blend well. Sprinkle with the sesame oil and serve.

Hot-and-Sour Pork

This tasty dish is cooked in the oven and uses less oil than a stir-fry. Trim all visible fat from the pork before cooking, for a healthy, low-fat recipe.

INGREDIENTS

Serves 4

12 ounces pork fillet
1 teaspoon sunflower oil
1-inch piece fresh ginger, grated
1 fresh red chili, seeded and
    finely chopped
1 teaspoon Chinese five-spice powder
1 tablespoon sherry vinegar
1 tablespoon soy sauce
1 can (8 ounces) pineapple chunks in
    natural juice
¾ cup chicken broth
4 teaspoons cornstarch
1 tablespoon water
1 green bell pepper, seeded and sliced
4 ounces baby corn, halved
salt and freshly ground black pepper
sprig of flat-leaf parsley, to garnish
boiled rice, to serve

1 Trim away any visible fat from the pork and cut into ½-inch-thick slices using a sharp knife.

2 Brush the sunflower oil over the base of a flameproof casserole. Heat over medium heat, then fry the pork for about 2 minutes on each side, or until lightly browned.

3 Blend together the ginger, chili, Chinese five-spice powder, sherry vinegar and soy sauce.

4 Drain the pineapple chunks, reserving the juice. Make the broth up to 1¼ cups by adding the reserved juice, mix together with the spices and pour over the pork.

5 Slowly bring the chicken broth to a boil. Blend the cornstarch with the water and gradually stir into the pork. Add the green bell pepper and baby corn and season to taste.

6 Cover and cook in a preheated oven at 325°F for 30 minutes, or until the pork is tender. Stir in the pineapple and cook for another 5 minutes. Garnish with flat-leaf parsley and serve with boiled rice.

COOK'S TIP

Chinese five-spice powder is available from Asian food stores and some large supermarkets. However, if you cannot find it, you can create your own by combining equal quantities of cinnamon, cloves, Szechuan peppercorns, fennel seeds and ground star anise or anise seeds.

Lion's Head Casserole

The name of this dish—*shi zi tou* in Chinese—derives from the rather strange idea that the meatballs look like a lion's head and the Chinese cabbage resembles its mane.

INGREDIENTS

Serves 4–6

1 pound ground pork
2 teaspoons finely chopped scallion
1 teaspoon finely chopped fresh ginger
2 ounces mushrooms, chopped
2 ounces cooked jumbo shrimp, peeled, or crabmeat, finely chopped
1 tablespoon light soy sauce
1 teaspoon light brown sugar
1 tablespoon Chinese rice wine or dry sherry
1 tablespoon cornstarch
1½ pounds Chinese cabbage

3–4 tablespoons vegetable oil
1 teaspoon salt
1¼ cups Basic Broth or water

1 Combine the pork, scallion, ginger, mushrooms, shrimp or crabmeat, soy sauce, sugar, rice wine or dry sherry and cornstarch. Shape the mixture into 4–6 meatballs.

2 Cut the Chinese cabbage into large pieces, all about the same size.

3 Heat the oil in a preheated wok or large frying pan. Add the Chinese cabbage and salt and stir-fry for 2–3 minutes. Add the meatballs and the broth or water, bring to a boil, cover and simmer gently for 30–45 minutes. Serve immediately.

Stir-fried Pork with Tomatoes and Zucchini

This dish is a perfect example of the Chinese way of balancing and harmonizing colours, flavors and textures.

INGREDIENTS

Serves 4

4 ounces firm tomatoes, skinned
6 ounces zucchini
1 scallion
8 ounces pork fillet, thinly sliced
1 tablespoon light soy sauce
1 teaspoon light brown sugar
1 teaspoon Chinese rice wine or dry sherry
2 teaspoons cornstarch paste
4 tablespoons vegetable oil
1 teaspoon salt (optional)
Basic Broth or water, if necessary

1 Cut the tomatoes and zucchini into wedges. Slice the scallion. Put the pork in a bowl with 1 teaspoon of the soy sauce, the sugar, rice wine or dry sherry and cornstarch paste. Set aside to marinate.

2 Heat the oil in a preheated wok and stir-fry the pork for 1 minute, or until it colors. Remove with a slotted spoon, set aside and keep warm.

3 Add the vegetables to the wok and stir-fry for 2 minutes. Add the salt, the pork and a little broth or water, if necessary, and stir-fry for 1 minute. Add the remaining soy sauce, mix well and serve.

Char-siu Pork

Marinated pork, roasted and glazed with honey, is irresistible on its own and can also be used as the basis for salads or stir-fries.

INGREDIENTS

Serves 6
1 tablespoon vegetable oil
1 tablespoon hoisin sauce
1 tablespoon yellow bean sauce
¼ teaspoon Chinese five spice powder
½ teaspoon cornstarch
1 tablespoon superfine sugar
1 pound lean pork, trimmed
2 teaspoons clear honey
salt and freshly ground white pepper
shredded scallion, to garnish
boiled rice, to serve

1 Mix together the vegetable oil, hoisin sauce, yellow bean sauce, Chinese five spice powder, cornstarch, and sugar in a shallow dish and season to taste with salt and pepper. Add the pork to the dish and turn to coat in the marinade thoroughly. Cover and chill for 4 hours.

2 Preheat the oven to 375°F. Drain the pork and place it on a wire rack over a deep roasting pan. Roast for 40 minutes, turning the pork over from time to time.

3 Check that the pork is cooked by inserting a fork into the meat; the juices should run clear. If they are still tinged with pink, roast the pork for a further 5–10 minutes.

4 Remove the pork from the oven and brush it with the honey. Allow to cool for 10 minutes before cutting into thin slices. Transfer to a serving dish, garnish with shredded scallion, and serve either hot or cold with boiled rice.

Stir-fried Pork with Lychees

Crispy pieces of pork with fleshy lychees make an unusual stir-fry that is ideal for a dinner party.

INGREDIENTS

Serves 4
1 pound fatty pork, such as pork belly
2 tablespoons hoisin sauce
4 scallions, sliced
6 heavy lychees, peeled, pitted and cut
  into slivers
salt and ground black pepper
lychees and fresh parsley sprigs, to
  garnish

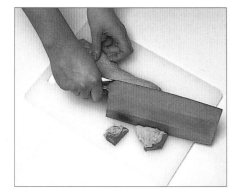

1 Using a cleaver or sharp knife, cut the pork into bite-sized pieces.

2 Pour the hoisin sauce over the pork and marinate for 30 minutes.

3 Heat a wok, then add the pork and stir-fry for 5 minutes, until crisp and golden. Add the scallions and stir-fry for another 2 minutes.

4 Scatter the lychee slivers over the pork, and season well with salt and pepper. Garnish with fresh lychees and parsley, and serve.

COOK'S TIP

If you cannot buy fresh lychees, this dish can be made with drained canned lychees.

Spicy Meat Fritters

INGREDIENTS

Makes 30

1 pound potatoes, boiled and drained
1 pound lean ground beef
1 onion, quartered
1 bunch scallions, chopped
3 garlic cloves, crushed
1 teaspoon ground nutmeg
1 tablespoon coriander seeds, dry-fried
   and ground
2 teaspoons cumin seeds, dry-fried
   and ground
4 eggs, beaten
oil for shallow-frying
salt and freshly ground black pepper

1 While the potatoes are still warm, mash them in the pan until they are well broken up. Add to the ground beef and mix well together.

2 Finely chop the onion, scallions and garlic. Add to the meat with the ground nutmeg, coriander and cumin. Stir in enough beaten egg to give a soft consistency which can be formed into fritters. Season to taste.

3 Heat the oil in a large frying pan. Using a dessertspoon, scoop out 6–8 oval-shaped fritters and drop them into the hot oil. Allow to set, so that they keep their shape (this will take about 3 minutes) and then turn over and cook for another minute.

4 Drain well on paper towels and keep warm while cooking the remaining fritters.

Barbecued Pork Spareribs

INGREDIENTS

Serves 4

2¼ pounds pork spareribs
1 onion
2 garlic cloves
1 inch fresh ginger root
⅓ cup dark soy sauce
1–2 fresh red chilies, seeded
   and chopped
1 teaspoon tamarind pulp, soaked in
   ⅓ cup water
1–2 tablespoons dark brown sugar
2 tablespoons peanut oil
salt and freshly ground black pepper

1 Wipe the pork ribs and place them in a wok, wide frying pan or large flameproof casserole.

2 Finely chop the onion, crush the garlic and peel and slice the ginger. Blend the soy sauce, onion, garlic, ginger and chopped chilies together to a paste in a food processor or with a mortar and pestle. Strain the tamarind and reserve the juice. Add the tamarind juice, brown sugar, oil and seasoning to taste to the onion mixture and mix well together.

3 Pour the sauce over the ribs and toss well to coat. Bring to a boil and then simmer, uncovered and stirring frequently, for 30 minutes. Add extra water if necessary.

4 Put the ribs on a rack in a roasting pan, place under a preheated broiler, on a barbecue grill or in the oven at 400°F. Continue cooking until the ribs are tender, about 20 minutes, depending on the thickness of the ribs. Baste the ribs with the sauce and turn them over from time to time.

Braised Birthday Noodles with Hoisin Lamb

In China, the egg symbolizes continuity and fertility so it is frequently included in birthday dishes. The noodles traditionally served at birthday celebrations are left long: it is considered bad luck to cut them as this might shorten one's life.

INGREDIENTS

Serves 4
12 ounces thick egg noodles
2¼ pounds lamb cutlets
2 tablespoons vegetable oil
4 ounces fine green beans, ends
   removed and blanched
salt and freshly ground black pepper
2 hard-boiled eggs, halved, and
   2 scallions, finely chopped, to garnish

For the marinade
2 garlic cloves, crushed
2 teaspoons grated fresh ginger
2 tablespoons soy sauce
2 tablespoons rice wine
1–2 dried red chilies
2 tablespoons vegetable oil

For the sauce
1 tablespoon cornstarch
2 tablespoons soy sauce
2 tablespoons rice wine
grated rind and juice of ½ orange
1 tablespoon hoisin sauce
1 tablespoon wine vinegar
1 teaspoon light brown sugar

1 Bring a large saucepan of water to a boil. Add the noodles, and cook for 2 minutes only. Drain, rinse under cold water, and drain again. Set aside.

2 Cut the lamb into 2-inch thick medallions. Mix the ingredients for the marinade in a large, shallow dish. Add the lamb, and marinate for at least 4 hours or overnight.

3 Heat the oil in a heavy-bottomed saucepan or flameproof casserole. Fry the lamb for 5 minutes until browned. Add just enough water to cover the meat. Bring to a boil, skim, then reduce the heat, and simmer for 40 minutes or until the meat is tender, adding more water as necessary.

4 Make the sauce. Blend the cornstarch with the remaining ingredients in a bowl. Stir into the lamb, and mix well without breaking up the meat.

5 Add the noodles to the lamb with the beans. Simmer gently until both the noodles and the beans are cooked. Add salt and pepper to taste. Divide the noodles, lamb and beans among four large bowls, garnish each portion with half a hard-cooked egg, sprinkle with scallions and serve.

Five-Spice Lamb

This mouthwatering and aromatic lamb dish is perfect for an informal supper party.

INGREDIENTS

Serves 4

2 tablespoons oil, plus more if needed
3–3½ pounds leg of lamb, boned
  and cubed
1 onion, chopped
2 teaspoons grated fresh ginger
1 garlic clove, crushed
1 teaspoon Chinese five-spice powder
2 tablespoons hoisin sauce
1 tablespoon light soy sauce
1¼ cups tomato paste
1 cup lamb or beef broth
1 red bell pepper, seeded and diced
1 yellow bell pepper, seeded and diced
2 tablespoons chopped fresh cilantro
1 tablespoon sesame seeds, toasted
salt and freshly ground black pepper
boiled rice, to serve

1 Heat the oil in a flameproof casserole and brown the lamb in batches over high heat. Remove and set aside.

2 Add the onion, ginger and garlic to the casserole with a little more oil, if necessary, and cook for about 5 minutes, until softened.

3 Return the lamb to the casserole. Stir in the five-spice powder, hoisin and soy sauces, tomato paste, broth and seasoning. Bring to a boil, cover and cook in a preheated oven at 325°F for 1¼ hours.

4 Remove the casserole from the oven, stir in the bell peppers, then cover and return to the oven for another 15 minutes, or until the lamb is cooked and very tender.

5 Sprinkle with the cilantro and sesame seeds. Serve hot with rice.

Peking Beef and Bell Pepper Stir-fry

This quick and easy stir-fry is perfect for today's busy cook and tastes superb.

INGREDIENTS

Serves 4

12 ounces sirloin steak, sliced into strips
2 tablespoons soy sauce
2 tablespoons medium sherry
1 tablespoon cornstarch
1 teaspoon light brown sugar
1 tablespoon sunflower oil
1 tablespoon sesame oil
1 garlic clove, finely chopped
1 tablespoon grated fresh ginger
1 red bell pepper, seeded and sliced
1 yellow bell pepper, seeded and sliced
4 ounces sugar snap peas
4 scallions, cut into 2-inch lengths
2 tablespoons oyster sauce
4 tablespoons water
cooked noodles, to serve

1 In a bowl, mix together the steak strips, soy sauce, sherry, cornstarch, and brown sugar. Cover and marinate for 30 minutes.

2 Heat the sunflower and sesame oils in a preheated wok or large frying pan. Add the garlic and ginger and stir-fry for about 30 seconds. Add the bell peppers, sugar snap peas and scallions and stir-fry for 3 minutes.

3 Add the beef, together with the marinade juices, to the wok or frying pan and stir-fry for another 3–4 minutes. Pour in the oyster sauce and water and stir until the sauce has thickened slightly. Serve immediately with cooked noodles.

Beef with Cantonese Oyster Sauce

This is a classic Cantonese recipe in which any combination of vegetables can be used. Broccoli may be used instead of snow peas, bamboo shoots instead of baby corn, and white or black mushrooms instead of straw mushrooms, for example.

INGREDIENTS

Serves 4
10–12 ounces sirloin steak
1 teaspoon light brown sugar
1 tablespoon light soy sauce
2 teaspoons Chinese rice wine or
  dry sherry
2 teaspoons cornstarch paste
4 ounces snow peas
4 ounces baby corn
4 ounces straw mushrooms
1 scallion
1¼ cups vegetable oil
few small pieces of fresh ginger
½ teaspoon salt
2 tablespoons oyster sauce

1 Cut the beef into thin strips. Place in a bowl and add the sugar, soy sauce, rice wine or dry sherry and cornstarch paste. Mix well and marinate for 25–30 minutes.

2 Trim the snow peas and cut the baby corn in half. If using canned straw mushrooms, drain them. If the straw mushrooms are large, cut them in half, but leave whole if they are small. Cut the scallion into short sections.

3 Heat the oil in a preheated wok and stir-fry the beef until the color changes. Remove with a slotted spoon and drain.

4 Pour off the excess oil, leaving about 2 tablespoons in the wok, then add the scallion, ginger and vegetables. Stir-fry for about 2 minutes with the salt, then add the beef and the oyster sauce. Blend well and serve.

Beef with Peppers and Black Bean Sauce

A rich dish with the distinctive flavour of black bean sauce.

INGREDIENTS

Serves 4

12 ounces sirloin steak, trimmed and
 thinly sliced
1 tablespoon vegetable oil
1¼ cups beef broth
2 garlic cloves, finely chopped
1 teaspoon grated fresh root ginger
1 fresh red chili, seeded and finely
 chopped
1 tablespoon black bean sauce
1 green bell pepper, seeded and cut
 into 1 inch squares
1 tablespoon dry sherry
1 teaspoon cornstarch
1 teaspoon superfine sugar
3 tablespoons cold water
salt
rice noodles, to serve

1 Place the steak in a bowl. Add 1 teaspoon of oil and stir to coat.

2 Bring the broth to a boil in a saucepan. Add the beef and cook for 2 minutes, stirring constantly to prevent the slices from sticking together. Drain the beef and set aside.

***

COOK'S TIP

For extra color, use half each of a green pepper and red pepper or a mixture that includes yellow and orange.

***

3 Heat the remaining oil in a non-stick frying pan or wok. Stir-fry the garlic, ginger and chili with the black bean sauce for a few seconds. Add the bell pepper squares and a little water. Cook for 2 minutes more, then stir in the sherry. Add the beef slices to the pan and spoon the sauce over.

4 In a small bowl, mix the cornstarch and sugar to a paste with the water. Pour the mixture into the pan. Cook, stirring, until the sauce has thickened. Season with salt and serve at once, with rice noodles.

Beef in Oyster Sauce

The oyster sauce gives the beef extra richness and depth of flavor. To complete the dish, all you need is plain boiled rice or simply cooked noodles.

INGREDIENTS

Serves 4
12 ounces lean steak, thinly sliced
1 tablespoon vegetable oil
1¼ cups beef stock
2 garlic cloves, finely chopped
1 small carrot, thinly sliced
3 celery stalks, sliced
1 tablespoon Chinese rice wine
1 teaspoon superfine sugar
3 tablespoons oyster sauce
1 teaspoon cornstarch
1 tablespoon water
4 scallions, cut into
   1-inch lengths
freshly ground white pepper
rice or noodles, to serve

1 Place the steak in a bowl, add 1 teaspoon of the oil and stir well.

2 Bring the stock to a boil in a large saucepan. Add the steak and cook, stirring constantly, for 2 minutes. Drain, reserving 3 tablespoons of the stock, and set aside.

3 Heat the remaining oil in a preheated wok. Stir-fry the garlic for a few seconds, then add the carrot and celery, and stir-fry for 2 minutes.

4 Stir in the Chinese rice wine, superfine sugar, and oyster sauce and season with pepper. Add the steak to the wok, together with the reserved stock. Simmer for 2 minutes.

5 Mix together the cornstarch and water to a smooth paste. Add the mixture to the wok and cook, stirring constantly, until thickened.

6 Stir in the scallions. Transfer to a warm serving dish and serve at once with plain boiled rice or noodles.

Asian Beef

This sumptuous stir-fried beef melts in the mouth, and is perfectly complemented by the delicious crunchy relish.

INGREDIENTS

Serves 4
1 pound sirloin steak
1 tablespoon sunflower oil
4 whole radishes, to garnish

For the marinade
2 garlic cloves, crushed
¼ cup dark soy sauce
2 tablespoons dry sherry
2 teaspoons dark brown sugar

For the relish
6 radishes
4-inch piece cucumber
1-inch piece preserved ginger

1 Cut the beef into thin strips. Place in a bowl.

2 To make the marinade, combine the garlic, soy sauce, sherry and sugar in another bowl. Pour it over the beef and let marinate overnight in the refrigerator.

COOK'S TIP

Dark soy sauce has a stronger, more robust flavour than light soy sauce. It is particularly useful for imparting a rich, dark colour to meat dishes.

3 To make the relish, chop the radishes and cucumber into short matchsticks, then cut the ginger into small matchsticks. Combine thoroughly in a bowl.

4 Heat a wok, then add the oil. When the oil is hot, add the meat and the marinade and stir-fry for 3–4 minutes. Serve with the relish, and garnish with a whole radish on each plate.

Mandarin Sesame Duck

Duck is a high-fat meat, but it is possible to get rid of a considerable proportion of the fat by cooking it in this way. (If you remove the skin completely, the meat can be dry.) For a special occasion, duck breasts are an excellent choice, but they are more expensive than legs.

INGREDIENTS

Serves 4
4 duck legs or boneless breasts
2 tablespoons light soy sauce
3 tablespoons honey
1 tablespoon sesame seeds
4 mandarin oranges
1 teaspoon cornstarch
salt and freshly ground black pepper
mixed vegetables, to serve

1 Prick the duck skin all over. If using breasts, slash the skin diagonally at intervals with a small, sharp knife.

2 Place the duck on a rack in a roasting pan and roast for 1 hour in a preheated oven at 350°F. Combine 1 tablespoon of the soy sauce with 2 tablespoons of the honey and brush over the duck. Sprinkle with sesame seeds. Roast for 15–20 minutes, or until golden brown.

3 Meanwhile, grate the rind from one mandarin and squeeze the juice from that one plus one other. Combine the rind, juice and cornstarch, then stir in the remaining soy sauce and honey. Heat, stirring, until thickened and clear. Season to taste. Peel and slice the remaining mandarins. Serve the duck with the mandarin slices, sauce and mixed vegetables.

Peking Duck

This has to be the *pièce de résistance* of any Chinese banquet. It is not too difficult to prepare and cook at home—the secret is to use duckling with a low fat content. Also, make sure that the skin of the duck is absolutely dry before you start to cook—the drier the skin, the crispier the duck.

INGREDIENTS

Serves 6–8

5–5¼ pounds oven-ready duckling
2 tablespoons honey, dissolved in
⅔ cup warm water

For the duck sauce

2 tablespoons sesame oil
6–8 tablespoons yellow bean sauce, crushed
2–3 tablespoons light brown sugar

To serve

20–24 Thin Pancakes
6–8 scallions, thinly shredded
½ cucumber, thinly shredded

COOK'S TIP

If preferred, serve Peking Duck with plum sauce in place of the duck sauce. Plum sauce is available from Asian stores and larger supermarkets. Duck sauce can also be bought ready-made.

1 Remove any feather studs and any lumps of fat from inside the vent of the duck. Plunge the duck into a saucepan of boiling water for 2–3 minutes to seal the pores. This will make the skin airtight, thus preventing the fat from escaping during cooking. Remove the duck and drain well, then dry thoroughly.

2 Brush the duck all over with the dissolved honey, then hang the bird up in a cool place for at least 4–5 hours.

3 Place the duck, breast side up, on a rack in a roasting pan and cook in a preheated oven at 400°F for 1½–1¾ hours without either basting or turning.

4 Meanwhile, make the duck sauce. Heat the sesame oil in a small saucepan. Add the crushed yellow bean sauce and the light brown sugar. Stir until smooth and allow to cool.

5 To serve, peel off the crispy duck skin in small slices using a sharp carving knife or cleaver, then carve the juicy meat in thin strips. Arrange the skin and meat on separate serving plates.

6 Open a pancake on each plate and spread about 1 teaspoon of the chosen sauce in the middle, with a few strips of shredded scallion and cucumber. Top with 2–3 slices each of duck skin and meat. Roll up and eat.

Sweet-and-sour Duck with Mango

Mango adds natural sweetness to this colorful stir-fry. Crispy deep-fried noodles make the perfect accompaniment.

INGREDIENTS

Serves 4

3 duck breasts (8–12 ounces total)
3 tablespoons dark soy sauce
1 tablespoon Chinese rice wine or
 dry sherry
1 teaspoon sesame oil
1 teaspoon five-spice powder
1 tablespoon brown sugar
2 teaspoons cornstarch
3 tablespoons Chinese rice vinegar
1 tablespoon ketchup
1 mango, not too ripe
3 baby eggplants
1 red onion
1 carrot
¼ cup peanut oil
1 garlic clove, sliced
1-inch piece fresh ginger, cut into shreds
3 ounces sugar-snap peas

1 Thinly slice the duck breasts and place in a bowl. Combine 1 tablespoon of the soy sauce with the rice wine or sherry, sesame oil and five-spice powder. Pour it over the duck, cover and let marinate for 1–2 hours. In a separate bowl, blend the sugar, cornstarch, rice vinegar, ketchup and remaining soy sauce. Set aside.

2 Peel the mango, slice the flesh from the pit, then cut into thick strips. Slice the eggplants, onion and carrot into similar-size pieces.

3 Heat a wok until hot, add 2 tablespoons of the oil and swirl it around. Drain the duck, reserving the marinade. Stir-fry the duck slices over high heat until the fat is crisp and golden. Remove and keep warm. Add 1 tablespoon of the oil to the wok and stir-fry the eggplants for 3 minutes until golden.

4 Add the remaining oil and fry the onion, garlic, ginger and carrot for 2–3 minutes, then add the sugar-snap peas and stir-fry for another 2 minutes.

5 Add the mango and return the duck with the sauce and reserved marinade to the wok. Cook, stirring, until the sauce thickens slightly. Serve immediately.

COOK'S TIP

If baby eggplants are not available, use the smallest eggplants you can find. Sprinkle with salt after slicing and set aside in a colander for the bitter juices to drain off. Rinse thoroughly before cooking.

Chicken with Lemon Sauce

Succulent chicken with a refreshing lemony sauce and just a hint of lime is a sure winner.

INGREDIENTS

Serves 4

4 small skinless chicken breasts fillets
1 teaspoon sesame oil
1 tablespoon Chinese rice wine
1 egg white, lightly beaten
2 tablespoons cornstarch
1 tablespoon vegetable oil
salt and freshly ground white pepper
cilantro leaves, scallions and lemon
   wedges, to garnish

For the sauce

3 tablespoons lemon juice
2 tablespoons lime cordial
3 tablespoons superfine sugar
2 teaspoons cornstarch
6 tablespoons water

1 Arrange the chicken breasts in a single layer in a shallow bowl. Mix together the sesame oil and Chinese rice wine and season with salt and pepper. Pour over the chicken, cover, and set aside in a cool place to marinate for about15 minutes.

2 Mix together the egg white and cornstarch. Add the mixture to the chicken and turn the chicken with tongs until it is thoroughly coated. Heat the vegetable oil in a preheated wok or skillet. Add the chicken fillets and fry, turning occasionally, for about 15 minutes, until golden brown on both sides.

3 Meanwhile, make the sauce. Combine all the ingredients in a small pan and season with salt. Bring to a boil over low heat, stirring constantly, until the sauce is smooth and has thickened slightly.

4 Cut the chicken into bite-size pieces and arrange them on a warm serving plate. Pour the lemon sauce over, garnish with the cilantro leaves, scallions, and lemon wedges and serve at once.

Salt "Baked" Chicken

The salt crust seals in all the delicious, succulent juices, keeping the chicken moist—yet the flavor is not salty.

INGREDIENTS

Serves 8
3–3½ pounds corn-fed chicken
¼ teaspoon sea salt
5 pounds coarse rock salt
1 tablespoon vegetable oil
1-inch piece fresh ginger root,
   finely chopped
4 scallions, cut into thin rings
boiled rice, garnished with shredded
   scallions, to serve

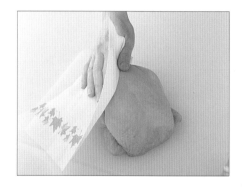

1 Rinse the chicken and pat dry, inside and out, with kitchen towels. Rub the inside with the sea salt.

2 Place four pieces of damp kitchen towel on the base of a heavy-based wok or skillet just large enough to hold the chicken.

3 Sprinkle a layer of rock salt over the kitchen towels, about ½-inch thick. Place the chicken on top.

4 Pour the remaining salt over the chicken until it is completely covered. Dampen six more pieces of kitchen towels and place them around the rim of the wok or skillet. Cover with a tight-fitting lid. Put the wok or skillet over high heat for about 10 minutes, or until it gives off a slightly smoky smell.

5 Immediately reduce the heat to medium and continue to cook the chicken for 30 minutes without lifting the lid. Then turn off the heat and leave for a further 10 minutes before carefully lifting the chicken out of the salt. Brush off any salt still clinging to the chicken and allow it to cool for 20 minutes before cutting it into serving-size pieces.

6 Heat the oil in a small saucepan until it is very hot. Add the ginger and scallions and fry for a few seconds, then pour into a heatproof bowl, and use as a dipping sauce for the chicken. Transfer the chicken to a warm serving plate and serve immediately with boiled rice, garnished with shredded scallions.

Chicken and Cashew Stir-fry

Hoisin sauce lends a sweet yet slightly hot note to this chicken stir-fry, while cashews add a pleasing contrast of texture.

INGREDIENTS

Serves 4

$^1/_2$ cup cashews
1 red bell pepper
1 pound boneless chicken breasts
3 tablespoons peanut oil
4 garlic cloves, finely chopped
2 tablespoons Chinese rice wine or dry sherry
3 tablespoons hoisin sauce
2 teaspoons sesame oil
5–6 scallions, green part only, cut into 1-inch lengths

2 Cut the red bell pepper in half and remove the seeds. Slice into thin strips. Skin the chicken fillet and cut into thin finger-length strips.

4 Add the rice wine or sherry and hoisin sauce. Continue to stir-fry until the chicken is tender and all the ingredients are evenly glazed.

1 Heat a wok until hot, add the cashews and dry-fry over low to medium heat for 1–2 minutes, until golden brown. Remove and set aside.

3 Heat the wok again until hot, add the oil and swirl it around. Add the garlic and let it sizzle in the oil for a few seconds. Add the bell pepper and chicken and stir-fry for 2 minutes.

5 Stir in the sesame oil, toasted cashews and scallions. Serve immediately.

COOK'S TIP

Use blanched almonds instead of cashews, if you prefer. For a slightly less sweet taste, you could substitute light soy sauce for the hoisin sauce.

Fu-yung Chicken

Because the egg whites mixed with milk are deep-fried in a wok, some imaginative cooks call this dish "Deep-fried Milk"!

INGREDIENTS

Serves 4

1 boneless chicken breast (about 6 ounces), skinned
1 teaspoon salt
4 egg whites, lightly beaten
1 tablespoon cornstarch paste
2 tablespoons milk
vegetable oil, for deep-frying
1 lettuce heart, separated into leaves
about ½ cup stock
1 tablespoon Chinese rice wine or dry sherry
1 tablespoon green peas
few drops of sesame oil
1 teaspoon diced ham, to garnish

1 Finely mince the chicken meat, then mix with a pinch of the salt, the egg whites, cornstarch paste and milk. Blend well until smooth.

2 Heat the oil in a very hot wok, but before the oil gets too hot, gently spoon the chicken and egg white mixture into the oil in batches. Do not stir, otherwise it will scatter. Stir the oil from the bottom of the wok so that the egg whites will rise to the surface. Remove as soon as the color turns bright white. Drain.

3 Pour off the excess oil, leaving about 1 tablespoon in the wok. Stir-fry the lettuce leaves with the remaining salt for 1 minute, add the stock and bring to a boil.

4 Add the chicken to the wok with the wine or sherry and peas, and blend well. Sprinkle with sesame oil, garnish with diced ham and serve.

Stir-fried Turkey with Snow Peas

Turkey is often a rather disappointing meat with a bland flavor. Here it is enlivened with a delicious marinade and combined with crunchy nuts to provide contrasting textures.

INGREDIENTS

Serves 4

2 tablespoons sesame oil
6 tablespoons lemon juice
1 garlic clove, crushed
½-inch piece fresh ginger, grated
1 teaspoon honey
1 pound turkey fillets, skinned and cut into strips
4 ounces snow peas
2 tablespoons peanut oil
2 ounces cashews
6 scallions, cut into strips
1 can (8 ounces) water chestnuts, drained and thinly sliced
salt
saffron rice, to serve

3 Drain the marinade from the turkey strips and reserve the marinade. Heat the peanut oil in a preheated wok or large frying pan, add the cashews and stir-fry for 1–2 minutes, or until golden brown. Remove the cashews from the wok or frying pan using a slotted spoon, and set aside.

4 Add the turkey to the wok or frying pan and stir-fry for 3–4 minutes, or until golden brown. Add the scallions, snow peas, water chestnuts and reserved marinade. Cook for a few minutes, until the turkey is tender and the sauce is bubbling and hot. Stir in the cashews and serve with saffron rice.

1 Combine the sesame oil, lemon juice, garlic, ginger and honey in a shallow, nonmetallic dish. Add the turkey and mix well. Cover and marinate for 3–4 hours.

2 Blanch the snow peas in boiling salted water for 1 minute. Drain, refresh under cold running water and set aside.

VEGETABLES

Stir-fried Greens

Quail's eggs look very attractive in *Chah Kang Kung*, but you can substitute some baby corn, halved at an angle.

INGREDIENTS

Serves 4

2 bunches spinach or chard or 1 head
   Chinese cabbage
3 garlic cloves, crushed
2 inches fresh ginger root, peeled and
   cut in matchsticks
3–4 tablespoons peanut oil
14 ounces boneless, skinless chicken
   breast, or pork loin, or a mixture of
   both, very finely sliced
12 quail's eggs, hard-boiled and shelled
1 fresh red chili, seeded and shredded
2–3 tablespoons oyster sauce
1 tablespoon brown sugar
2 teaspoons cornstarch, mixed with
   ¼ cup cold water
salt

COOK'S TIP

As with all stir-fries, don't start cooking until you have prepared all the ingredients and arranged them to hand. Cut everything into small, even-size pieces so the food can be cooked very quickly and all the colors and flavors preserved.

1 Wash the chosen leaves well and shake them dry. Strip the tender leaves from the stems and tear them into pieces. Discard the lower, tougher part of the stems and slice the remainder evenly.

2 Fry the garlic and ginger in the hot oil, without browning, for a minute. Add the chicken and/or pork and keep stirring it in the wok until the meat changes color. When the meat looks cooked, add the sliced stems first and cook them quickly; then add the torn leaves, quail's eggs and chili. Spoon in the oyster sauce and a little boiling water, if necessary. Cover and cook for 1–2 minutes only.

3 Remove the lid, stir and add sugar and salt to taste. Stir in the cornstarch and water mixture and toss thoroughly. Cook until the mixture is well coated in a glossy sauce.

4 Serve immediately, while still very hot and the colors are bright and glowingly jewel-like.

Stir-fried Chinese Cabbage

This really simple way of cooking Chinese cabbage perfectly preserves the delicate flavor, texture and color of this classic vegetable.

INGREDIENTS

Serves 4

1½ pounds Chinese cabbage
1 tablespoon vegetable oil
2 garlic cloves, finely chopped
1-inch piece fresh ginger root, finely chopped
1 tablespoon oyster sauce
4 scallions, cut into 1-inch lengths
salt

1 Stack the cabbage leaves together and cut them into 1-inch slices with a sharp knife.

2 Heat the oil in a preheated wok or heavy-based skillet. Add the garlic and ginger and stir-fry for 1 minute.

3 Add the Chinese cabbage leaves and stir-fry for 2 minutes. Sprinkle with salt and drizzle with the oyster sauce. Toss the leaves over the heat for a further 2 minutes.

4 Stir in the scallions. Toss the mixture well, transfer to a warm serving plate, and serve.

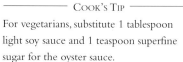

COOK'S TIP

For vegetarians, substitute 1 tablespoon light soy sauce and 1 teaspoon superfine sugar for the oyster sauce.

Mixed Vegetables Monk-style

Chinese monks eat neither fish nor meat, so "monk-style" dishes are fine for vegetarians.

INGREDIENTS

Serves 4

2 ounces dried bean curd sticks
4 ounces fresh lotus root or 2 ounces dried
¼ ounce dried wood ears
8 dried Chinese mushrooms
1 tablespoon vegetable oil
¾ cup drained, canned straw mushrooms
1 cup baby corn cobs, cut in half
2 tablespoons light soy sauce
1 tablespoon Chinese rice wine
2 teaspoons superfine sugar
⅔ cup vegetable stock
3 ounces snow peas, trimmed and cut in half
1 teaspoon cornstarch
1 tablespoon water
salt

1 Put the bean curd sticks in a bowl. Cover with hot water and set aside to soak for 1 hour. If using fresh lotus root, peel and slice it. If using dried lotus root, place it in a bowl of hot water and set aside to soak for 1 hour.

2 Soak the wood ears and dried mushrooms in separate bowls of hot water for 15 minutes. Drain the wood ears, trim off and discard the hard base from each, and cut the rest into bite-size pieces. Drain the mushrooms, trim off and discard the hard stems, and chop the caps roughly.

3 Drain the bean curd sticks. Cut them into 2-inch long pieces, discarding any hard pieces. If using dried lotus root, drain well.

4 Heat the oil in a preheated wok or skillet. Add the wood ears, Chinese mushrooms, and lotus root and stir-fry for about 30 seconds.

5 Add the pieces of bean curd sticks, straw mushrooms, baby corn cobs, soy sauce, rice wine, sugar, and stock. Bring to a boil, cover, lower the heat, and simmer for about 20 minutes.

6 Stir in the snow peas and season to taste with salt. Mix together the cornstarch and water to a smooth paste. Add the mixture to the wok or skillet and cook, stirring constantly, until the sauce thickens. Serve at once.

Szechuan Eggplants

INGREDIENTS

Serves 4

2 small eggplants
1 teaspoon salt
3 dried red chilies
peanut oil, for deep-frying
3–4 garlic cloves, finely chopped
½-inch piece fresh ginger, finely
   chopped
4 scallions, chopped and white and
   green parts separated
1 tablespoon Chinese rice wine or
   dry sherry
1 tablespoon light soy sauce
1 teaspoon sugar
¼ teaspoon ground roasted
   Szechuan peppercorns
1 tablespoon rice vinegar
1 teaspoon sesame oil

1 Trim the eggplants and cut into strips about 1½ inches wide and 3 inches long. Place the eggplants in a colander and sprinkle with the salt. Let sit for 30 minutes, then rinse them thoroughly under cold running water. Pat dry with paper towels.

2 Meanwhile, soak the chilies in warm water for 15 minutes. Drain, then cut each chili into three or four pieces, discarding the seeds.

3 Half-fill a wok with oil and heat to 350°F. Deep-fry the eggplants, in batches if necessary, until golden brown. Drain on paper towels. Pour off most of the oil from the wok. Reheat the oil and add the garlic, ginger and white part of the scallions.

4 Stir-fry for 30 seconds. Add the eggplants and toss, then add the wine or sherry, soy sauce, sugar, ground peppercorns and vinegar. Stir-fry for 1–2 minutes. Sprinkle on the sesame oil and scallion greens.

Root Vegetables with Spiced Salt

All kinds of root vegetables can be finely sliced and deep fried to make "chips." Serve as an accompaniment to an Asian-style meal or simply by themselves as much tastier nibbles than store-bought snacks with predinner drinks.

INGREDIENTS

Serves 4–6
1 carrot
2 parsnips
2 raw beets
1 sweet potato
peanut oil, for deep-frying
¼ teaspoon chili powder
1 teaspoon sea salt flakes

1 Peel the carrot, parsnips, beets and sweet potato. Slice the carrot and parsnips into long, thin ribbons. Cut the beets and sweet potato into thin rounds. Pat dry with paper towels.

2 Half-fill a wok with oil and heat to 350°F. Add the vegetable slices in batches and deep-fry for 2–3 minutes, until golden and crisp. Remove and drain on paper towels.

3 Place the chili powder and sea salt flakes in a mortar and grind them together with a pestle to form a coarse powder.

4 Pile the vegetable "chips" on a serving plate and sprinkle with the spiced salt.

— COOK'S TIP —

To save time, you can slice the vegetables using a mandoline, blender or food processor with a thin slicing disc attached.

Red-cooked Tofu with Chinese Mushrooms

"Red-cooked" is a term applied to Chinese dishes cooked with a dark soy sauce. This tasty dish can be served as either a side dish or a main course.

INGREDIENTS

Serves 4

8-ounce package fresh firm tofu
3 tablespoons dark soy sauce
2 tablespoons Chinese rice wine or
   dry sherry
2 teaspoons dark brown sugar
1 garlic clove, crushed
1 tablespoon grated fresh ginger
½ teaspoon five-spice powder
pinch of ground roasted Szechuan
   peppercorns
6 dried black Chinese mushrooms
1 teaspoon cornstarch
2 tablespoons peanut oil
5–6 scallions, sliced into 1-inch lengths,
   white and green parts separated
small fresh basil leaves, to garnish
rice noodles, to serve

2 Meanwhile, soak the dried black mushrooms in warm water for 30 minutes, until soft. Drain, reserving 6 tablespoons of the soaking liquid. Squeeze out any excess liquid from the mushrooms, remove the tough stalks and slice the caps. In a small bowl, blend the cornstarch with the reserved marinade and mushroom soaking liquid.

4 Add the mushrooms and white parts of the scallions to the wok and stir-fry for 2 minutes. Pour in the reserved marinade and stir for 1 minute, until thickened.

5 Return the tofu to the wok with the green parts of the scallions. Simmer gently for 1–2 minutes. Scatter the basil leaves on top and serve immediately with rice noodles.

1 Drain the tofu, pat dry with paper towels and cut into 1-inch cubes. Place in a shallow dish. In a small bowl, combine the soy sauce, rice wine or sherry, sugar, garlic, ginger, five-spice powder and Szechuan peppercorns. Pour the marinade over the tofu, toss well and let marinate for about 30 minutes. Drain, reserving the marinade.

3 Heat a wok until hot, add the oil and swirl it around. Add the tofu and stir-fry for 2–3 minutes, until evenly golden. Remove from the wok and set aside.

Braised Chinese Vegetables

The original recipe calls for no fewer than 18 different ingredients to represent the 18 Buddhas (*lo han*). Later, this was reduced to eight, but nowadays anything between four and six items is regarded as quite sufficient to put in a wok.

INGREDIENTS

Serves 4

¼ cup dried Chinese mushrooms
1 cup straw mushrooms
½ cup sliced bamboo shoots, drained
2 ounces snow peas
3-inch block fresh tofu
6 ounces bok choy leaves
3–4 tablespoons vegetable oil
1 teaspoon salt
½ teaspoon light brown sugar
1 tablespoon light soy sauce
few drops of sesame oil

1 Soak the Chinese mushrooms in warm water for 30 minutes, then rinse and discard the hard stalks, if any. Cut the straw mushrooms in half lengthwise if they are large; keep them whole if they are small. Rinse and drain the bamboo-shoot slices. Trim the snow peas. Cut the tofu into about 12 small pieces. Cut the bok choy into small pieces about the same size as the snow peas.

2 Harden the tofu pieces by placing them in a wok of boiling water for about 2 minutes. Remove and drain.

3 Discard the water and heat the oil in the wok, a saucepan or a flameproof casserole. Lightly brown the tofu pieces on both sides. Remove with a slotted spoon and keep warm.

4 Stir-fry all the vegetables in the wok for 1½ minutes, then add the tofu, salt, sugar and soy sauce. Continue stirring for 1 minute, then cover and braise for 2–3 minutes. Sprinkle with sesame oil and serve.

Stir-fried Bean Sprouts

This is an easy way to cook up some tasty bean sprouts in a wok. It is not necessary to trim them. Simply rinse in a bowl of cold water and discard any husks that float to the surface.

INGREDIENTS

Serves 4
2–3 scallions
3 tablespoons vegetable oil
2 cups bean sprouts
1 teaspoon salt
½ teaspoon light brown sugar
few drops of sesame oil (optional)

1 Cut the scallions into short sections about the same length as the bean sprouts.

2 Heat the oil in a wok and stir-fry the bean sprouts and scallions for about 1 minute. Add the salt and sugar and continue stirring for 1 minute. Sprinkle with the sesame oil, if using, and serve. Do not overcook, or the bean sprouts will become soggy.

COOK'S TIP

Fresh and canned bean sprouts are readily available, but they can easily be grown at home for a constant and completely fresh supply. Scatter mung beans on several layers of damp paper towels on a small plate. Keep moist in a fairly warm place, and the beans will sprout in a few days.

Pancakes with Stir-fried Vegetables

To serve, each person spreads a little hoisin sauce over a pancake, adds a helping of the filling from the wok and rolls up the pancake.

INGREDIENTS

Serves 4

3 eggs
2 tablespoons water
¼ cup peanut oil
¼ cup dried black Chinese mushrooms
¼ cup dried wood ear mushrooms
2 teaspoons cornstarch
2 tablespoons light soy sauce
2 tablespoons Chinese rice wine or
   dry sherry
2 teaspoons sesame oil
2 garlic cloves, finely chopped
½-inch piece fresh ginger, cut into
   thin shreds
½ cup canned sliced bamboo shoots,
   drained and rinsed
½ cup bean sprouts
4 scallions, finely shredded
salt and ground black pepper
fresh cilantro, to garnish
Chinese pancakes and hoisin sauce,
   to serve

1 Whisk the eggs, water and seasoning in a small bowl. Heat 1 tablespoon of the peanut oil in a wok and swirl it around. Pour in the eggs, then tilt the wok so that they spread into an even layer. Continue to cook over high heat for about 2 minutes, until set. Turn onto a board and, when cool, roll up the omelet and cut into thin strips. Wipe the wok clean.

— COOK'S TIP —

Chinese pancakes are available at Asian supermarkets. Reheat them in a bamboo steamer for 2–3 minutes just before serving.

2 Meanwhile, put the black Chinese mushrooms and wood ear mushrooms in separate bowls. Pour in enough warm water to cover, then let soak for 30 minutes, until soft. Drain the mushrooms, reserving their soaking liquid. Squeeze the excess liquid from each of them.

3 Remove the tough stalks and thinly slice the black mushrooms. Finely shred the wood ears. Set aside. Strain the reserved soaking liquid through cheesecloth into a bowl; reserve ½ cup of the liquid. In a bowl, blend the cornstarch with the reserved liquid, soy sauce, rice wine or sherry and sesame oil.

4 Heat the wok over medium heat, add the remaining peanut oil and swirl it around. Add the wood ears and black mushrooms and stir-fry for about 2 minutes. Add the garlic, ginger, bamboo shoots and bean sprouts and stir-fry for 1–2 minutes.

5 Pour in the cornstarch mixture and cook, stirring, for 1 minute, until thickened. Add the scallions and omelet strips and toss gently. Adjust the seasoning, adding more soy sauce, if needed. Serve immediately with the Chinese pancakes, garnished with cilantro, and accompanied by the hoisin sauce.

RICE &
NOODLES

Chinese Special Fried Rice

This recipe combines a tasty mixture of chicken, shrimp and vegetables with fried rice.

INGREDIENTS

Serves 4

scant 1 cup long-grain white rice
3 tablespoons peanut oil
1½ cups water
1 garlic clove, crushed
4 scallions, finely chopped
4 ounces cooked chicken, diced
4 ounces cooked jumbo shrimp, peeled
2 ounces frozen peas
1 egg, lightly beaten
2 ounces lettuce, shredded
2 tablespoons light soy sauce
pinch of superfine sugar
salt and freshly ground black pepper
1 tablespoon chopped roasted cashews,
   to garnish

1 Rinse the rice in two to three changes of warm water to wash away some of the starch. Drain well.

2 Put the rice in a saucepan and add 1 tablespoon of the oil and the water. Cover and bring to a boil, stir once, then cover and simmer for 12–15 minutes, until nearly all the water has been absorbed. Turn off the heat and cover; let stand for 10 minutes. Fluff up with a fork and let cool.

3 Heat the remaining oil in a preheated wok or frying pan, add the garlic and scallions and stir-fry for 30 seconds.

4 Add the chicken, shrimp and peas and stir-fry for 1–2 minutes, then add the cooked rice and stir-fry for another 2 minutes. Pour in the egg and stir-fry until just set. Stir in the lettuce, soy sauce, sugar and seasoning.

5 Transfer to a warmed serving bowl, sprinkle with the chopped cashews and serve immediately.

Chinese Jeweled Rice

This rice dish, with its many different, interesting ingredients, is practically a meal in itself.

INGREDIENTS

Serves 4

1½ cups long-grain rice
3 tablespoons vegetable oil
1 onion, roughly chopped
4 ounces cooked ham, diced
6-ounce can white crabmeat
½ cup water chestnuts, drained and cut into cubes
4 dried black Chinese mushrooms, soaked, drained and diced
½ cup green peas, thawed if frozen
2 tablespoons oyster sauce
1 teaspoon sugar
salt

1 Rinse the rice, then cook for 10–12 minutes in 3–3¾ cups salted water in a saucepan with a tight-fitting lid. When cooked, refresh under cold water. Heat half the oil in a preheated wok, then stir-fry the rice for 3 minutes. Remove and set aside.

2 Add the remaining oil to the wok. When the oil is hot, cook the onion until softened but not colored.

3 Add all the remaining ingredients and stir-fry for 2 minutes.

4 Return the rice to the wok and stir-fry for 3 minutes, then serve.

Shiitake Fried Rice

Shiitake mushrooms have a strong, meaty aroma and flavor. This is a very easy recipe to make, and although it is a side dish, it can almost be a meal in itself.

INGREDIENTS

Serves 4

2 eggs
1 tablespoon water
3 tablespoons vegetable oil
12 ounces shiitake mushrooms
8 scallions, sliced diagonally
1 garlic clove, crushed
½ green bell pepper, seeded and
  chopped
2 tablespoons butter
about 1 cup long-grain rice, cooked
1 tablespoon medium-dry sherry
2 tablespoons dark soy sauce
1 tablespoon chopped fresh cilantro
salt

1 Beat the eggs with the water and season with a little salt.

2 Heat 1 tablespoon of the oil in a preheated wok or large frying pan, pour in the eggs and cook to make a large omelet. Lift the sides of the omelet and tilt the wok so that the uncooked egg can run underneath and be cooked. Roll up the omelet and slice thinly.

3 Remove and discard the mushroom stalks, if they are tough. Slice the caps thinly, halving them if they are large.

4 Heat 1 tablespoon of the oil in the wok and stir-fry the scallions and garlic for 3–4 minutes, until softened but not brown. Transfer them to a plate using a slotted spoon and set aside.

5 Add the green bell pepper and stir-fry for about 2–3 minutes, then add the butter and the remaining oil. As the butter begins to sizzle, add the mushrooms and stir-fry over moderate heat for 3–4 minutes, or until both vegetables are soft.

6 Loosen the rice grains as much as possible. Pour the sherry over the mushrooms and then stir in the rice.

7 Heat the rice over moderate heat, stirring all the time to prevent it from sticking. If the rice seems very dry, add a little more oil. Stir in the cooked scallions, garlic and omelet slices, the soy sauce and the chopped cilantro. Cook for a few minutes, until heated through, and serve.

Chicken Chow Mein

Chow Mein is arguably the best known Chinese noodle dish in the West. To make it, noodles are stir-fried with meat, seafood or vegetables.

INGREDIENTS

Serves 4

12 ounces noodles
8 ounces skinless, boneless chicken
   breasts
3 tablespoons soy sauce
1 tablespoon rice wine or dry sherry
1 tablespoon dark sesame oil
4 tablespoons vegetable oil
2 garlic cloves, finely chopped
2 ounces snow peas, ends removed
4 ounces bean sprouts
2 ounces ham, finely shredded
4 scallions, finely chopped
salt and freshly ground black pepper

1 Cook the noodles in a saucepan of boiling water until tender. Drain, rinse under cold water, and drain well.

2 Slice the chicken into fine, 2-inch shreds. Place in a bowl. Add 2 teaspoons of the soy sauce, the rice wine or sherry and sesame oil.

3 Heat half the vegetable oil in a wok or large frying pan over a high heat. When the oil starts smoking, add the chicken mixture. Stir-fry for about 2 minutes, then transfer the chicken to a plate, and keep it hot.

4 Wipe the wok clean, and heat the remaining oil. Stir in the garlic, snow peas, bean sprouts and ham, stir-fry for another minute or so, and add the noodles.

5 Continue to stir-fry until the noodles are heated through. Add the remaining soy sauce to taste, and season with salt and pepper. Return the chicken and any juices to the noodle mixture, add the scallions, and give the mixture a final stir. Serve at once.

Sesame Duck and Noodle Salad

This salad is complete in itself and makes a lovely summer lunch. The marinade is a marvelous blend of spices.

INGREDIENTS

Serves 4

2 duck breasts
1 tablespoon vegetable oil
2 medium carrots, cut into 3-inch sticks
5 ounces sugar snap peas
8 ounces medium egg noodles
6 scallions, sliced
salt
fresh cilantro leaves, to garnish

For the marinade

1 tablespoon sesame oil
1 teaspoon ground coriander
1 teaspoon Chinese five-spice powder

For the dressing

1 tablespoon garlic vinegar
1 teaspoon light brown sugar
1 teaspoon soy sauce
1 tablespoon toasted sesame seeds
freshly ground black pepper
3 tablespoons sunflower oil
2 tablespoons sesame oil

1 Slice the duck breasts thinly crosswise and place them in a shallow dish. Combine the ingredients for the marinade, pour over the duck and mix well to coat thoroughly. Cover and let sit in a cool place for 30 minutes.

2 Heat the oil in a preheated wok or frying pan, add the slices of duck breast and stir-fry for 3–4 minutes, or until cooked. Set aside.

3 Bring a saucepan of lightly salted water to a boil. Place the carrots and sugar snap peas in a steamer that will fit on top of the pan. When the water boils, add the noodles, place the steamer on top and steam the vegetables while cooking the noodles

for the time suggested on the package. Set the steamed vegetables aside. Drain the noodles, refresh them under cold running water and drain again. Place them in a large serving bowl.

4 To make the dressing, mix the vinegar, sugar, soy sauce and sesame seeds in a bowl. Season well with black pepper, then whisk in the sunflower and sesame oils.

5 Pour the dressing over the noodles and mix well. Add the sugar snap peas, carrots, scallions and duck slices and toss to combine. Scatter the cilantro leaves on top and serve.

Asian Vegetable Noodles

Thin Italian egg pasta is a good alternative to Asian egg noodles; use it fresh or dried.

INGREDIENTS

Serves 6

1¼ pounds thin tagliarini
4 ounces shiitake mushrooms
1 red onion
3 tablespoons sesame oil
3 tablespoons dark soy sauce
1 tablespoon balsamic vinegar
2 teaspoons superfine sugar
salt
celery leaves, to garnish

1 Cook the tagliarini in a large pan of salted boiling water, following the instructions on the package.

2 Thinly slice the mushrooms and the red onion, using a sharp knife.

3 Heat 1 tablespoon of the sesame oil in a preheated wok. When the oil is hot, stir-fry the onion and mushrooms for 2 minutes.

4 Drain the tagliarini, then add to the wok with the soy sauce, balsamic vinegar, sugar and salt to taste. Stir-fry for 1 minute, then add the remaining sesame oil and serve garnished with celery leaves.

Peanut Noodles

Add any of your favorite vegetables to this recipe to make a great, quick midweek supper— and increase the chili, if you can take the heat!

INGREDIENTS

Serves 4

7 ounces medium egg noodles
2 tablespoons olive oil
2 garlic cloves, crushed
1 large onion, roughly chopped
1 red bell pepper, seeded and roughly chopped
1 yellow bell pepper, seeded and roughly chopped
12 ounces zucchini, roughly chopped
1¼ cups roasted unsalted peanuts, roughly chopped

For the dressing

¼ cup olive oil
grated rind and juice of 1 lemon
1 fresh red chili, seeded and finely chopped
4 tablespoons chopped fresh chives
1–2 tablespoons balsamic vinegar
salt and freshly ground black pepper

1 Cook the noodles according to the package instructions and drain well.

2 Meanwhile, heat the oil in a preheated wok or very large frying pan and cook the garlic and onion for 3 minutes, or until beginning to soften. Add the bell peppers and zucchini and cook for another 15 minutes over medium heat, until beginning to soften and brown. Add the peanuts and cook for 1 minute more.

3 For the dressing, whisk together the olive oil, grated lemon rind and 3 tablespoons lemon juice, the chili, 3 tablespoons of the chives, plenty of seasoning and balsamic vinegar to taste.

4 Toss the noodles into the vegetables and stir-fry to heat through. Add the dressing, stir to coat and serve immediately, garnished with the remaining chopped fresh chives.

Chinese Mushrooms with Cellophane Noodles

Red fermented bean curd adds extra flavor to this hearty vegetarian dish. It is brick-red in color, with a very strong flavor of cheese, and is made by fermenting bean curd (tofu) with salt, red rice and rice wine. Look out for it in cans or jars at Chinese food markets.

INGREDIENTS

Serves 4

4 ounces dried Chinese mushrooms
1 ounce dried wood ears
4 ounces dried bean curd
2 tablespoons vegetable oil
2 garlic cloves, finely chopped
2 slices fresh ginger, finely chopped
10 Szechuan peppercorns, crushed
1 tablespoon red fermented bean curd
½ star anise
pinch of sugar
1–2 tablespoons soy sauce
2 ounces cellophane noodles, soaked in
   hot water until soft
salt

2 Strain the mushrooms, reserving the liquid. Squeeze as much liquid from the mushrooms as possible, then discard the mushroom stems. Cut the cups in half if they are large.

5 Add the reserved mushroom liquid to the pan, with sufficient water to cover the mushrooms completely. Add the star anise, sugar and soy sauce, then cover, and simmer for 30 minutes.

6 Add the chopped wood ears and reconstituted bean curd pieces to the pan. Cover, and cook for about 10 minutes.

7 Drain the cellophane noodles, add them to the mixture, and cook for 10 minutes more until tender, adding more liquid if necessary. Add salt to taste, and serve.

1 Soak the Chinese mushrooms and wood ears separately in bowls of hot water for 30 minutes. Break the dried bean curd into small pieces, and soak in water according to the instructions on the package.

3 The wood ears should swell to five times their original size. Drain, rinse thoroughly, and drain again. Cut off any gritty parts, and cut each wood ear into two or three pieces.

4 Heat the oil in a heavy-bottomed pan. Add the garlic, ginger and Szechuan peppercorns. Fry for a few seconds, then add the mushrooms and red fermented bean curd. Mix lightly, and fry for 5 minutes.

COOK'S TIP

If you can't find Szechuan peppercorns, then use ordinary black ones instead.

Fried Cellophane Noodles

INGREDIENTS

Serves 4

6 ounces cellophane noodles
3 tablespoons vegetable oil
3 garlic cloves, finely chopped
4 ounces cooked shrimp, peeled
2 lap cheong, rinsed, drained and
    finely diced
2 eggs
2 celery stalks, including leaves, diced
4 ounces bean sprouts
4 ounces spinach, cut into large pieces
2 scallions, chopped
1–2 tablespoons fish sauce
1 teaspoon sesame oil
1 tablespoon sesame seeds, toasted,
    to garnish

1 Soak the cellophane noodles in hot water for about 10 minutes or until soft. Drain, and cut the noodles into 4-inch lengths.

2 Heat the oil in a wok, add the garlic, and fry until golden brown. Add the shrimp and lap cheong. Stir-fry for 2–3 minutes. Stir in the noodles, and fry for 2 minutes more.

3 Make a well in the center of the shrimp mixture, break in the eggs, and slowly stir them until they are creamy and just set.

— COOK'S TIP —

This is a very versatile dish. Vary the vegetables if you wish, and substitute ham, chorizo or salami for the lap cheong.

4 Stir in the celery, bean sprouts, spinach and scallions. Season with fish sauce, and stir in the sesame oil. Continue to stir-fry until all the ingredients are cooked, mixing well.

5 Transfer to a serving dish. Sprinkle with sesame seeds to garnish.

DESSERTS

Chinese Fruit Salad

For an unusual fruit salad with an Asian flavor, try this mixture of fruits in a tangy lime and lychee syrup, topped with a light sprinkling of toasted sesame seeds.

INGREDIENTS

Serves 4
½ cup superfine sugar
1¼ cups water
thinly pared rind and juice of 1 lime
1 can (14 ounces) lychees in syrup
1 ripe mango, peeled, pitted and sliced
1 eating apple, cored and sliced
2 bananas, chopped
1 star fruit, sliced (optional)
1 teaspoon sesame seeds, toasted

1 Place the sugar in a saucepan with the water and the lime rind. Heat gently until the sugar dissolves, then increase the heat and boil gently for about 7–8 minutes. Remove from the heat and set aside to cool.

2 Drain the lychees and reserve the juice. Pour the juice into the cooled lime syrup with the lime juice. Place all the prepared fruit in a bowl and pour the lime and lychee syrup over it. Chill for about 1 hour. Just before serving, sprinkle with toasted sesame seeds.

COOK'S TIP

To prepare a mango, cut through the fruit lengthwise, about ½ inch either side of the center. Then, using a sharp knife, cut the flesh from the central piece from the pit. Make even crisscross cuts in the flesh of both side pieces. Hold one side piece in both hands, bend it almost inside out and remove the cubes of flesh with a spoon. Repeat with the other side piece.

Thin Pancakes

Thin pancakes are not too difficult to make, but quite a lot of practice and patience are needed to achieve the perfect result. Nowadays, even restaurants buy frozen, ready-made ones from Chinese supermarkets. If you decide to use ready-made pancakes, or are reheating home-made ones, steam them for about five minutes, or microwave on high for one to two minutes.

INGREDIENTS

Makes 24–30
4 cups all-purpose flour, plus extra for dusting
about 1¼ cups boiling water
1 teaspoon vegetable oil

1 Sift the flour into a mixing bowl, then pour in the boiling water very gently, stirring as you pour. Mix with the oil and knead the mixture into a firm dough. Cover with a damp cloth and let stand for about 30 minutes.

2 Lightly dust a work surface with flour. Knead the dough for 5–8 minutes, or until smooth, then divide it into three equal portions. Roll out each portion into a long "sausage," cut each into eight to ten pieces and roll each into a ball. Using the palm of your hand, press each piece into a flat pancake. With a rolling pin, gently roll each into a 6-inch circle.

3 Heat an ungreased frying pan until hot, then reduce the heat to low and place the pancakes, one at a time, in the pan. Remove the pancakes when small brown spots appear on the underside. Keep under a damp cloth until all the pancakes are cooked.

Red Bean Paste Pancakes

If you are unable to find red bean paste, sweetened chestnut purée or mashed dates are possible substitutes.

INGREDIENTS

Serves 4
about 8 tablespoons sweetened red bean paste
8 Thin Pancakes
2–3 tablespoons vegetable oil
granulated or superfine sugar, to serve

1 Spread about 1 tablespoon of the red bean paste over about three-quarters of each pancake, then roll the pancake over three or four times.

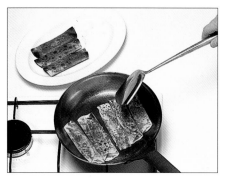

2 Heat the oil in a preheated wok or frying pan and fry the pancake rolls until golden brown, turning once.

3 Cut each pancake roll into three or four pieces and sprinkle with sugar to serve.

Almond Curd Junket

Also known as almond float, this dessert is usually made with agar or isinglass, although gelatin can also be used.

INGREDIENTS

Serves 4–6

¼ ounce agar or 1 ounce gelatin
   powder
about 2½ cups water
4 tablespoons superfine sugar
1¼ cups milk
1 teaspoon almond extract
fresh or canned mixed fruit salad with
   syrup, to serve

1 In a saucepan, dissolve the agar in about half the water over gentle heat. This will take at least 10 minutes. (If using gelatin, follow the package instructions.)

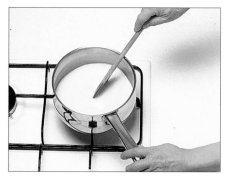

2 In a separate saucepan, dissolve the sugar in the remaining water over medium heat. Add the milk and the almond extract, blending well. Do not allow the mixture to boil.

3 Mix the milk and sugar with the agar or gelatin mixture in a serving bowl. When cool, place in the refrigerator for 2–3 hours to set.

4 To serve, cut the junket into small cubes and spoon into a serving dish or into individual bowls. Pour the fruit salad, with the syrup, over the junket and serve.

Toffee Apples

Enjoy all the flavor and texture of this classic Chinese dessert without the fuss, and high fat, of deep-frying.

INGREDIENTS

Serves 6
2 tablespoon butter
5 tablespoons water
6 tablespoons all-purpose flour
1 egg
1 dessert apple
1 teaspoon vegetable oil
¾ cup superfine sugar
1 teaspoon sesame seeds

1 Preheat the oven to 400°F. Put the butter and water into a small saucepan and bring to a boil. Remove from the heat and add the flour all at once. Stir vigorously until the mixture forms a smooth paste which leaves the sides of the pan clean.

2 Cool the choux paste for 5 minutes, then beat in the egg, mixing thoroughly until the mixture is smooth and glossy.

3 Peel and core the apple and cut it into ½-inch chunks. Stir into the choux paste and place teaspoonfuls on a dampened, non-stick cookie sheet. Bake for 20–25 minutes, until brown and crisp on the outside, still soft inside.

4 Heat the oil in a saucepan over low heat and add the superfine sugar. Cook, without stirring, until the sugar has melted and turned golden brown. Sprinkle in the sesame seeds and remove the pan from the heat.

5 Have a bowl of ice water at hand. Add the apple pastries, a few at a time, to the caramel and toss thoroughly to coat them all over. Remove with a slotted spoon and quickly dip them in the ice water to set the caramel. Drain well, transfer to a serving dish, and serve at once. If the caramel becomes too thick before all the apple pastries have been coated, re-heat it gently over low heat until it liquifies again.

INDEX